Thames
and Downs
by Rail

A guide to the routes,
scenery and towns

ABOUT THIS BOOK

Thames and Downs by Rail is one of a series of guide-books compiled by the Railway Development Society, the independent voluntary body for rail-users.

We invite you to explore the heart of Southern England by train, with some suggestions for further excursions from various railheads by bus, boat, bicycle, or on foot.

As Editor, I should like to thank all the members of the RDS who have written knowledgeably and interestingly about their local lines; the Thames & Chilterns Tourist Board and individual photographers for illustrations; Stephen Binks for the line diagrams and Christopher Jones for the map; Simon Norton and Nicholas Hammond for providing additional information; Geoffrey Roper for help with proof-reading.

A few points on railway background will help you to appreciate the book fully and obtain greatest interest and enjoyment from your travels.

The up line is the track used by trains travelling towards London; the down line being the opposite.

The Great Western Railway and the London & South Western Railway were the two private companies which built or operated most lines in this region. Other companies operating in those days, and referred to in the text, include the South Eastern, Great Central, London & North Western, and London, Brighton & South Coast.

The rails on almost all British lines are 4 feet 8½ inches apart – which is known as 'standard gauge'; but the Great Western Railway was originally built with rails 7 feet apart, known as 'broad gauge', and not fully converted to standard gauge until 1892.

High Speed Trains, also known as 'InterCity 125s', are express diesel trains, with a power unit at either end, first introduced on British Rail in 1977. DMUs are diesel multiple units, also known as 'railcars', which operate most local services.

The private railway companies were nationalised as British Railways (later British Rail) in 1948. Dr Richard Beeching was Chairman of BR in the early 1960s and under his chairmanship scores of local lines and stations were closed.

Network South East is the name used by that sector of BR which operates most local passenger services in the region covered by this guide.

The line diagrams show all stations on routes described in the book. Those printed in capitals are major stations with a wide range of services and facilities; others are usually served only by local trains and may be unstaffed or only staffed for part of the day.

Every effort has been made to include up-to-date information, but we shall be pleased to receive any comments or corrections for incorporation in any future editions.

Trevor Garrod

Front cover: Charlbury Station. (*Photo:* M. D. Hull)
Back cover: Bridge of Sighs, Hertford College, Oxford.
Title page: The Thames at Marlow. (*Photo:* Roy J. Westlake, A.R.P.S.)

CONTENTS

About This Book	2
Editor's Introduction	4
London Paddington–Reading by Tim Young	5
Reading–Swindon–Bath by Martin Smith	6
Reading–Westbury by John Jackson	10
Coventry–Banbury–Thames Valley by Geoffrey Wyatt	12
Reading–Basingstoke by Sue Cooper	15
London Waterloo–Southampton by Jon Honeysett	16
Southampton–Poole by Colin Mortimer	20
Basingstoke–Salisbury by Norman Cox	24
London Waterloo–Portsmouth by Ken Wright	28
Portsmouth–Westbury (and Fareham–Eastleigh) by Jon Honeysett	31
Swindon–Westbury by Ian McGill	36
London Marylebone–Banbury by Derek Foster	39
London Marylebone–Aylesbury by Stephen Sykes	42
Oxford–Bicester Town by Nicholas Medley	45
Oxford–Worcester (The Cotswold line) by Oliver Lovell	46
Twyford–Henley on Thames by Sue Cooper	49
Maidenhead–Marlow by Nigel Hunt	50
Windsor by John Bye	52
Ascot/Guildford–Reading by Peter Scott	54
Mid Hants Railway (The Watercress line)	56
Isle of Wight by Paul Scott and Martin Heys	57
Brockenhurst–Lymington by Trevor Garrod	59
City of Southampton by Trevor Garrod	60
City of Portsmouth by Ken Wright	60
City of Oxford by Martin Smith	61
Further Information	63
What is the Railway Development Society?	64

Sandown Pier Pavilion. (*Photo:* Isle of Wight Tourist Office)

EDITOR'S INTRODUCTION

Chalky downland ridges, broad vales, and placid waterways; historic towns and cities and great tracts of heath and forest are shared by five counties in the heart of Southern England – Hampshire, Berkshire, Wiltshire, Oxfordshire, and Buckinghamshire.

From Oxford's dreaming spires to Romsey's massive Norman abbey; from Windsor's stately castle to Salisbury's soaring cathedral, a wealth of distinguished architecture awaits the traveller.

Boats abound – from Henley's world-famous Regatta on the majestic Thames to the forest of yachts on the winding Lymington River; from narrow barges on the restored Kennet & Avon Canal to the ocean-going giants that ply Southampton Water.

Mainline railways bring all these places within easy reach of London; while cross-country routes give access from the Midlands, Bristol, and South Wales. Over 600 miles of route serve these attractive southern shires.

High Speed Trains pass along the Thames Valley at up to 125 m.p.h.; frequent electrics whisk you down to Hampshire; diesel railcars afford panoramic views of the Chilterns out to Aylesbury or the charming byways to Marlow and Henley. For further variety, there are both vintage electrics and steam trains on the Isle of Wight; or the living museums at Didcot and Quainton Road, and even a narrow-gauge electric train along Hythe Pier.

Lines have been reopened to the market towns of Melksham and Bicester; new stations have been built to serve expanding communities at Winnersh, Hedge End, and Haddenham – and there is scope for more.

You can alight from some 160 stations and explore the region further – on foot through the New Forest, by bicycle through the Vales of Pewsey or White Horse; by steamer from Oxford, Henley, Marlow, or Windsor.

Whether on an excursion or a longer holiday, you will find much of interest and beauty as you explore these southern shires by rail.

Trevor Garrod

The restored Little Bedwyn Lock, alongside the Kennet Valley line. (*Photo:* Kennet & Avon Canal Trust)

LONDON PADDINGTON–READING
by Tim Young

Paddington Station, situated in Praed Street, just a few yards away from St Mary's Hospital, where Sir Alexander Fleming made his historic discovery of the drug penicillin, is where we commence our journey. Set well back from the road, it must be one of the most inconspicuous of London's mainline termini; that is until you arrive on the grand concourse, which at Paddington is referred to as 'The Lawn'. This handsome station, and the Great Western Railway itself, was designed by the eminent engineer Isambard Kingdom Brunel (1806–59). Do not miss the statue of the great man, sitting in his chair by the main exit from the Underground and contemplating his handiwork. Pause also long enough to admire the War Memorial on Platform 1, an attractive statue of a 'Tommy' from the First World War, and the more modern Paddington Bear in a glass case on 'The Lawn'.

Travellers to Reading will normally catch one of the frequent High Speed Trains which run to South Wales or the West Country and complete the 36 miles to Berkshire's county town in a little over twenty minutes, departing from one of the mainline Platforms 1 to 8. If travelling to one of the intermediate stations, you would normally leave from one of the local Platforms 9 to 14 and make the journey by DMU.

As you leave Paddington, you will notice the extensive parcels platforms to your left and the Hammersmith branch of the Metropolitan Line to your right, running on the surface. The A40 motorway runs alongside to the right on a flyover as you go past Royal Oak Station with Ranelagh Bridge fuelling point on your left.

By the next station, Westbourne Park, the London Transport lines have dived almost imperceptibly under the British Rail lines to reappear on the left and then curve sharply away southwards. Old Oak Common, the main locomotive depot serving Paddington, soon appears on the right and further junctions with lines to and from Olympia, High Wycombe, and the North London Line are passed.

After the next station, Acton Main Line, is a Foster Yeoman stone siding on the right. You may be lucky enough to see one of their four American-built Class 59 locomotives, which they bought to haul their own trains instead of using BR locos. Underground lines trail in on the right as we approach Ealing Broadway Station, an important interchange point with the District and Central lines.

After the next station, West Ealing, a single line curves off to the right, bound for Greenford, and the densely built suburbs gradually give way to more open country. The eight-arched Wharncliffe Viaduct spans the Brent Valley with its golf-courses, and soon the suburbs also become interspersed with stretches of water left by former gravel workings. At Iver Station, the M25, arguably the world's longest ring road, crosses the line.

The train crosses into Berkshire and soon reaches Slough, a station of particular historical importance since it was here, on 13 June 1842, that the first Royal Train ran in this country, conveying Queen Victoria and Prince Albert from Slough to

Paddington. Today one changes at Slough for a branch-line service to Windsor (described on page 53) and on the left Windsor Castle can be seen in the distance. Windsor's near neighbour, Eton, was not pleased by the arrival of the railway. The Headmaster of Eton College did not want his boys to even see the trains, let alone ride on them, and had a 10-foot-high wall built to screen the railway from his pupils' view. The annual Eton Wall game was subsequently developed, in which no one has scored a goal in over eighty years.

After the next station, Burnham, you briefly re-enter Buckinghamshire to pass through Taplow Station before crossing back into Berkshire over a bridge which is further testament to the skill of Brunel. When the line was constructed, the Thames Commissioners decreed that the river should remain navigable; so he designed a low flat brick-arched bridge which his critics felt would not withstand the weight of the trains passing over it. However, Maidenhead Bridge has survived to prove them wrong.

Maidenhead is the junction for Marlow (described on page 51) and is one of a number of pleasant towns that line this stretch of the Thames. On leaving it, our train is in open country and after the next station, Twyford, where the Henley branch (described on pages 49–50) goes off to the right, you enter the deep Sonning Cutting which had to be dug out by scores of navvies. One of the characteristics of Brunel's planning of the line was its lack of gradients. He aimed to keep it as flat as possible, and some even nicknamed it the 'Billiard Table line'.

We soon enter Reading, a busy town of 130,000 people on the bank of the Thames, which we see again alongside the line to the right. As you pull into Reading Station, notice on your left a red-brick square tower. This is Reading Gaol, of which Oscar Wilde wrote a famous ballad. He was one of the inmates, as was John Bunyan. The lines from the Southern route finally trail in to meet ours from the left as our train comes to a halt in Reading Station, currently being redeveloped and dwarfed by the Western Tower office block just across the road.

Reading is well worth exploring, with pleasant walks along the river-bank at Caversham and an extensive shopping centre just south of the station. Look at the Forbury Gardens (adjacent to the gaol) dominated by a large copper statue, which despite its grey colour is of a lion. Also in the gardens are the ruins of Reading Abbey, within whose bounds are buried the mortal remains of Henry I. There is a university, most of whose buildings are on a campus in Whiteknights Park on the eastern outskirts of the town. You are free to walk through the campus, on which there is an interesting Museum of English Rural Life.

READING–SWINDON–BATH
by Martin Smith

On leaving Reading Station, we see the Kennet Valley line to Newbury and the West Country curving sharply away to our left. Soon the Thames approaches close to the line on our right-hand side, and the railway follows the river closely for the next 9 miles through the picturesque Goring Gap, between the Chilterns and the Berkshire Downs. The first station is Tilehurst, serving a suburb of Reading.

The next station is Pangbourne, a popular riverside resort and highly desirable commuter village. We pass through a deep chalk cutting, and about a mile beyond Pangbourne, some unusual breeds of sheep and cattle can be seen grazing in meadows between the railway line and the river. These belong to the Child Beale Trust which owns the park farm and the ornamental gardens, open to the public, in the grounds of Basildon House.

The railway crosses the river into Oxfordshire, and we come to Goring and Streatley Station. For long-distance walkers this is a convenient starting-point for a walk westwards along the Ridgeway, or north-eastwards along the extension of the Ridgeway Path, following the Chiltern Escarpment. After passing through the village of South Stoke, we again cross the river over Moulsford Bridge, and come to Cholsey Station, formerly the junction for the Wallingford branch whose rusting rails can still be seen curving away to the right. A preservation group, formed to reopen the branch, has established a centre at Wallingford and acquired some rolling-stock.

As we travel westwards, a range of low hills comes into view on our right. These are the Sinodun Hills, with two prominent clumps of trees called Wittenham Clumps on top of the western end. The right-hand clump is planted within the rings of an Iron Age hill-fort, an outlier of the chain of forts extending along the Downs. Soon the massive cooling towers of Didcot power-station loom ahead, the abandoned track of the Didcot, Newbury & Southampton line comes in on the left, and we arrive at Didcot.

The town is a straggling, nondescript place which has grown up around Didcot Junction, since the railway to Oxford was opened in 1844. With the introduction of InterCity 125 trains, bringing Didcot within thirty-one minutes of Paddington, and the transmogrification of the station into a Parkway, Didcot has become a popular commuter town. Although the station was rebuilt in 1985, the two island platforms have kept their original awnings with ornamental valances; and with plenty of old GWR benches around, the station has kept some of its Great Western atmosphere.

Didcot is the home of the Great Western Railway Society's Steam Centre which occupies a restricted site between the Didcot avoiding line and the junction, into which an extensive layout has been fitted. There is a 'mainline' about ½ mile long, on which the mainline engines give short runs, and a 'branch line' serving 'Didcot Halt', which has a preserved corrugated-iron pagoda-style shelter typical of the old GWR. (Appleford Halt, 2 miles down the Oxford line, described on page 15, has its original shelters still in use.) An interesting feature is a section of broad-gauge and mixed-gauge track, running into a transfer shed, demonstrating how the problem of break of gauge was dealt with. The centre is open to the public most week-ends, but it is best to visit on steaming days – usually the first and last Sundays in each month and Bank Holiday Mondays, with extra dates in high summer.

Between Didcot and Swindon, the mainline runs through the Vale of White Horse, the scenery of which is being re-created in miniature, with a model of a typical village as it would have been in about 1930, at the Pendon Museum, Long Wittenham. The model village, called Pendon Parva, is fictitious, but every building is modelled on a real building from one of the villages in the Vale. The museum also includes an extensive model railway layout representing a Great Western scene in South Devon in the early 1900s. Pendon Museum is open from 2 to 5 p.m. on Saturdays and Sundays, and from 11 a.m. to 5 p.m. on Bank Holiday Mondays. The nearest access

Didcot Steam Centre, showing locomotives that used to head the trains west out of London Paddington. (*Photo:* Thames & Chilterns Tourist Board)

by public transport is to Appleford, from where it is a pleasant walk, in fine weather, of 1½ miles by footpath through the riverside meadows to Long Wittenham.

After leaving Didcot and passing the triangular junction with the Oxford line, we see two private sidings diverging on the right, the first leading into the power-station, and the second into Milton trading estate, an inland port served by continental ferry wagons. As we flash through the site of Steventon Station at 125 m.p.h., we can catch a glimpse of two handsome houses built by Brunel for the opening of the railway. In the early years this was an important station, being the nearest to Oxford, which was served by coaches connecting with the trains. Also, as Steventon was about half-way between London and Bristol, the Board of Directors of the Great Western Railway for a period held their weekly meetings here and suitable accommodation had to be provided.

The next disused station that we pass was at Wantage Road which, from 1875 to 1945, was connected by a roadside steam tramway to the town of Wantage, King Alfred's birthplace, 2½ miles away. After passing the site of Challow Station, we come to Uffington, formerly the junction for the Faringdon branch. The village, which was the home of Thomas Hughes, the author of *Tom Brown's Schooldays,* is on our left, with its octagonal church tower.

The Downs are now much closer to the left-hand side of the railway, and soon we can see the White Horse, carved by the Belgae, a Celtic tribe who lived here 2,000 years ago, just below the earthworks of Uffington Fort, whose outline can be discerned on the summit of the hill.

We soon enter the outskirts of Swindon. The arrival of the Great Western Railway in 1841 and the establishment of its works transformed, almost overnight, a small rural community of about 1,800 souls into a major nineteenth-century industrial town. The old town was at the top of the hill, about a mile from the station, but Brunel built a model new town for the workers in the locomotive and carriage works which were established here.

The railway works have passed into history, the local economy has diversified, but the town has not forgotten its heritage, for the borough of Thamesdown is custodian of the fine collection of exhibits housed at the Great Western Railway Museum, some ¼ mile from the station, at the corner of Bridge Street and Faringdon Road. The adjacent streets, which housed much of the works' labour force, have been sensitively restored and one dwelling, at No. 34 Faringdon Road, next to the railway museum, is open to the public.

Modern Swindon has a fine covered shopping centre, and many new industries are being established to replace the jobs lost with the closing of the railway works. Within easy reach of the town is the Thamesdown Museum's fine eighteenth-century house at Lydiard Tregoze, set in extensive parkland about 5 miles to the west, open Monday to Saturday. Take a Thamesdown No. 4 bus from Fleming Way at Stop 2. About 2 miles south-east is the Jeffries Museum and adjacent country park around Coate Water (frequent Thamesdown buses 8, 13, 14, and 15 from Fleming Way).

Swindon is the railhead for the important prehistoric site at Avebury (Thamesdown No. 49 bus; infrequent service) or the National Trust property at Ashdown Park, open Monday to Friday (a Thamesdown No. 47 bus takes you to the gates; infrequent service). Other rewarding excursions can be made to the Vale of White Horse, the North Wiltshire Downs, and the Upper Thames around Inglesham; the route of Service 47 across the Downs to Lambourn and Newbury is particularly recommended for its scenery. It is essential to confirm details of times and services of country buses before setting out. The principal operators are Swindon & District (telephone 0793–22243) and Thamesdown Transport (telephone 0793–23700).

About 4 miles south of Swindon is Wroughton Airfield, where the Science Museum keeps the greater part of its transport and agricultural machinery collections. It is open to the public on selected week-ends (telephone 0793–814466 for details). On the second Sunday in September an open day is held, when many of the exhibits are working, and vintage buses give rides round the airfield. On open days, a special bus service operates from Swindon bus station.

The line to Gloucester and Cheltenham, which was part of the mainline to South Wales before the opening of the Severn Tunnel, and which during the 1930s was the route of the famous 'Cheltenham Flyer', is now relegated to secondary status and, apart from three InterCity trains a day to London, is served by DMUs between Cheltenham and Swindon. Shortly after leaving Swindon, the line crosses over the track of the former Midland & South Western Junction Railway, part of which has been taken over by the Swindon & Cricklade Railway Society who have established a centre at Blunsdon Station, 4 miles north of Swindon. The first stop on the Gloucester line is Kemble, formerly the junction for the Tetbury and Cirencester branches. If we get off the train at Kemble, it is a walk of only a mile by footpaths to the source of the Thames at Thameshead, thus completing our journey by rail through the Thames Valley. Gloucester and Cheltenham themselves are described in our companion volume, *Midlands by Rail*.

Returning to the mainline, the disused railway works are on our right as we leave Swindon. At Wootton Bassett Junction, the South Wales direct line via Badminton, opened in 1903 and served by InterCity trains to Bristol Parkway, Cardiff, and Swansea, diverges on our right. We soon come into the valley of the River Avon and, as we approach Chippenham, the track of the disused Calne branch joins us on the left.

Chippenham is an interesting old market town described on page 37. Our train then crosses a high viaduct in the middle of the town. Two miles farther on, at Thingley Junction, the Trowbridge line diverges to our left, following the river, and our InterCity 125 veers to the right into the hills, over the most heavily engineered section of the line, through a 3-mile-long cutting past Corsham (where there is now a campaign to get the station reopened) followed by the 2-mile-long Box Tunnel. The tunnel is perfectly straight, on a falling gradient of 1 in 100 which caused considerable alarm to passengers in the early days who were afraid that trains might run away. It is said that on about 21 June, the rising sun shines right through the tunnel and can be seen from the west end before it rises above Box Hill. From Box the line winds steeply down through a narrow valley to meet the Avon again at Bathford, and then follows the river through Bath to Bristol. This section and the cities of Bath and Bristol are described in our companion volume *South West by Rail*.

READING–WESTBURY
by John Jackson

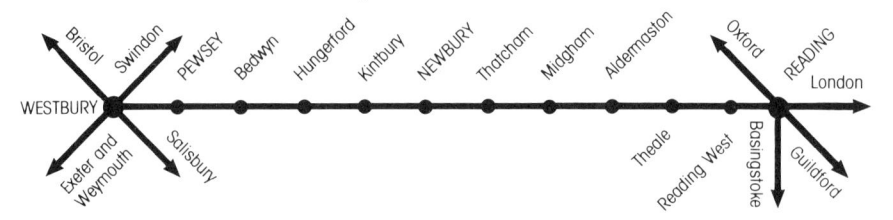

Brunel's original Great Western Railway from Paddington to Reading opened in 1840, as a prototype of railway development during the Victorian era. Today's InterCity 125 trains speed us westwards from Paddington to join the scenic Kennet line from Reading to Westbury, through the country of Sir Felix Pole, the great legendary Manager of the GWR in the inter-war period.

As we take our seat on a High Speed Train bound for the Cornish Riviera we may first begin reading MacDermot's classic *History of the Great Western Railway*, that Sir Felix commissioned in the heyday of 'God's Wonderful Railway'.

The City of London bearings on the Great Western crest directed Brunel via the lordly Thames Valley on his way west. He had been snookered by the lie of the land and opposition from the Kennet & Avon Canal between Reading and Bath, and this coloured his judgement to take a cushion shot on his 'Billiard Table' to Bristol via Swindon.

Subsequently, spurred on by competition from the London & South Western Railway's proposal for a line from Basingstoke to Bath, the Great Western moved in on the Kennet Valley after all, and opened this route in late 1847. It was a wise move, and 'The West was won' by the GWR, for today the clear Kennet route overtakes all others for time and amenity in travelling to the South West.

The route is closely related to the River Kennet, the Kennet & Avon Canal, and the A4 Great West Road along the wide reaches of the vale. Unless the reader is particularly interested in train-spotting, identifying rare birds among the wildfowl, or charting the velocity of our train from the ¼-mile posts (for simplicity divide 900 by the number of seconds taken between two such posts on the right-hand side), this is a suitable opportunity to partake of refreshment from the welcoming buffet car. Beverages, biscuits (preferably locally made Huntley & Palmers), hot meals, fruit, and rail ale will refresh our flagging spirits to prepare for the delights of the scenery soon to unfold.

Aldermaston, in recent times the target of anti-nuclear protests, also has the claim to fame of being the location of the GWR headquarters during the Second World War – the site, once the canal branch wharf, is now occupied by Sterling Cable. If you preferred to purchase a William pear for the fruit course, you may be interested to know that John Stair, a local schoolmaster in the 1770s, developed the William pear at Aldermaston in those green pre-nuclear days.

Between Aldermaston and Midgham, 560-yard-long water troughs once refreshed the GWR express engines here as they scooped up water into their tenders at speed. At Midgham for Douai School Station a new abbey church, begun in 1930, complements the flinty Midgham Church and spire to the north. The station was originally named after the adjacent village of Woolhampton until the Victorians confused it with Wolverhampton and were not amused.

As we pass Thatcham, it is of interest to consider the level crossings and Reed's paper factory at Colthrop. At the beginning of the nineteenth century, Colthrop papermills, on the left, were run by Fourdrinier, who invented the machinery for making paper in a continuous roll rather than in separate sheets. Today's continuous paper and packaging produced at Colthrop may well paper over the cracks of my scribbler's narrative.

Newbury, once a junction for Didcot, Lambourn, and Winchester, is now just another intermediate station — but it is in the centre of a busy town of 25,000 souls and, unlike the next three stations farther west, is fully staffed. On the northern outskirts of the town is Donnington Castle, knocked about a bit in the Civil War but now open to the public.

After Newbury the landscape undergoes subtle changes — the valley narrows and the Downs move in closer; we seem to have left 'Silicon Valley' and reached quieter, more pastoral country. The scenery compels us more to look out of the windows, less to browse in a book. There is parkland and woodland on the valley sides, while the canal waters are constantly visible to the south of the line.

Kintbury Station serves a picturesque village perched on the hillside on the other side of the water. If we are on a local train, we may feel like alighting here and strolling along the towpath or up into the hills.

A few miles farther on is Hungerford, whose broad main street, dominated by its Town Hall tower, runs down the hill, under the railway, and over the canal's humpbacked bridge. The Common to the south of the town is a pleasant spot to picnic; while *The Rose of Hungerford* offers enjoyable canal trips on summer week-ends (telephone 83873 for details). What better way to appreciate and support the work of volunteers of the Kennet & Avon Trust, whose ultimate aim is to restore for leisure purposes this waterway from Reading to Bristol with which the GWR first competed, a century and a half ago?

West of Hungerford, the line parts company with the main road and veers southwest into Wiltshire. The hills close in and the line curves its way between them in close company with the canal and a minor road. There is no station to serve the compact village of Little Bedwyn, with its eighteenth-century manor farmhouse, but there is one at Great Bedwyn, a mile farther west. Indeed, this neat and modest halt

The *Rose of Hungerford* in the Basin of the Kennet & Avon Canal, two minutes' walk from Hungerford Station. (Photo: Thames & Chilterns Tourist Board)

was Sir Felix Pole's local station. One wonders whether he would approve of the notice on the platform here telling would-be travellers to the West Country to catch a train 13½ miles eastwards to Newbury, and change there into a westbound High Speed Train. This curious instruction, also found at Hungerford Station, is because the local DMU service from Reading terminates at Bedwyn.

A mile farther on, the train passes Crofton pumping-station, on the right, built at the highest point on the canal to pump water into it from a nearby reservoir. It is open at week-ends and steamed once a month in summer. It can be reached by walking or cycling along a quiet lane from Great Bedwyn.

Our journey into Wiltshire continues along the southern flanks of Savernake Forest. Once there was a busy interchange station here with the north–south Midland & South Western Junction Railway and the branch to Marlborough. Now these lines and Savernake's two stations are 'one with Nineveh and Tyre', and only a few overgrown earthworks remain.

The Vale of Pewsey soon opens out before us and the canal finally meanders away to the north-west. Four InterCity trains each way call at Pewsey Station – serving a large village with a statue of Alfred the Great in its centre and a White Horse cut on the scarp of the Down behind it. The neat brick buildings of Pewsey Station were tastefully restored in 1985 as part of the 'GWR 150' celebrations and won an award for this. The station car park will probably be full, as Pewsey provides park-and-ride facilities for a wide rural area.

There are no more stations on the remaining 20¼-mile stretch of line to Westbury – but a case can be made for a Devizes Parkway Station 7½ miles west of Pewsey where the line passes just 2 miles south-east of the town of Devizes with its 15,000 people. A station car park and minibus service to the town would be provided and both tourists and local people would benefit.

The northern edge of Salisbury Plain now forms a continuous rampart to the south, with villages such as Lavington (which could also possibly justify a reopened station) at its foot. Presently we spot the church of Edington Priory to the south, commemorating King Alfred's victory over the Danes at Ethendune; and then the earthworks of Bratton Castle and the great White Horse of Westbury dominate the Down. We thus reach Westbury Station, 95½ miles from Paddington and seventy minutes by the fastest train on 'God's Wonderful Railway to the West'.

COVENTRY–BANBURY–THAMES VALLEY
by Geoffrey Wyatt

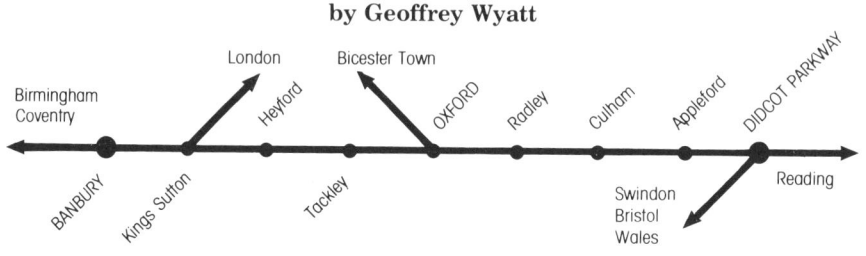

Trains to the Thames Valley and South Coast from as far afield as Liverpool, Manchester, Glasgow, and Newcastle pass down this line. They include a named express – the 'Wessex Scot' from Glasgow to Poole – as well as trains from Wolverhampton and Birmingham to Paddington which used to travel via High Wycombe but are now diverted to serve the large centres of population in the Thames Valley *en route* to the capital.

All of these trains serve Coventry, where we start our journey in the modern station.

We diverge from the Birmingham – Euston mainline on to the Leamington branch to our left. The passenger services on this 9½-mile link were withdrawn under the Beeching Plan, but in 1977 it became one of the first lines to reopen, to provide through services to the Solent and Thames Valley from Coventry and Birmingham International.

Since then, other lines and stations have reopened – indeed, 150 stations have reopened or been newly built on British Rail in the last twenty years – including Coventry – Nuneaton in May 1987. This latter route is now used by a through service from Nottingham and Leicester to Coventry, thus bringing these important cities of the East Midlands just one change of train away from the Thames Valley and the South Coast.

Although some of the Coventry – Leamington line was built as double track, the entire route was singled during its freight-only existence to facilitate construction of the Kenilworth bypass. This makes it difficult to reopen any stations between Coventry and Leamington because of its high level of occupancy by existing trains.

Leamington Spa, an elegant inland resort, and neighbouring Warwick with its great medieval castle are described in our companion volume *Midlands by Rail*. We climb out of Leamington and soon pass over the Roman road of Fosse Way. Then we see where passing loops once stood on either side of the mainline. Entering and emerging from a cutting, we see on our right Greaves cement works, which is still served by Railfreight.

The next point of interest comes at Fenny Compton, where we catch our first sighting of the Oxford Canal, which will rarely be far from our line for the next 30 miles. To the right is the last remaining stretch of the Stratford & Midland Junction Railway, serving the Ministry of Defence at Burton Dasset. On our left an embankment built by the Oxford & Rugby Railway never saw any track laid before the Great Western Railway took over and diverted the line to Leamington and Birmingham.

Cropredy, scene of the battle in 1644, is the next sizeable community. The canal comes close to the line on our left with the River Cherwell just beyond it. Then on the right is the Alcan factory and the formation of the former North Oxfordshire Ironstone Company Railway. We cross the canal and spot the formation of the former Great Central Railway link to Woodford Halse.

To our right is a reservoir and then we pass under two close bridges. To our right is the General Foods factory, home of Maxwell House Coffee and Birds Desserts. Then comes a view across the river and canal of Banbury town, with the Town Hall, bus station and, in the distance, St Mary's Church, before we pass under the A361 road bridge to run alongside the station's long platforms. The town of Banbury is described on page 42.

Leaving Banbury, we see Banbury United football ground and the site of the GWR locomotive shed on the right, while to the left is the gasometer, sewage works and, to the keen eyed, the formation of the former L&NWR line to Verney Junction.

Soon we cross from Oxfordshire into Northamptonshire, the River Cherwell, just to our right, forming the county boundary. Kings Sutton Station will be preceded by the locomotive or DMU horn, as access to and from the northbound platform is via an ungated crossing of the line. Kings Sutton was the junction for the rural Banbury – Cheltenham direct line, the unlikely route of the 'Port to Port Express'. The bridge that carried this line over the river and canal can still be seen.

Next comes Aynho, with its flyover junction for the direct line to Bicester and London. It was opened in 1910 and is known locally as the 'New Line'. The northbound platform building survives as a restaurant – the Great Western Arms, alas now serving only canal and road travellers. Beyond the junction we cross back into Oxfordshire and to our left is the impressive Souldern Viaduct.

Train near Kings Sutton. (*Photo:* John Baker)

The canal comes close in on our left, while the small village of Somerton is on the hillside to our right. Like Aynho, it, too, lost its station in the 1960s. Soon after is Upper Heyford, where there is a USAF base, the runway of which stretches almost between our line and the Bicester line but is visible from neither. A cutting is followed by a bridge over the river, and then we run parallel to the canal to Heyford Station. Like Tackley, 2¾ miles farther south, it is served by some seven local DMUs each way per day.

After Tackley we cross the river four times and the canal twice, before the remains of the Woodstock branch, serving Blenheim Palace, are discernible on the right. The River Cherwell soon meanders away to the left but the canal keeps company with the railway. To our right, but not visible, is Oxford Airport, followed by the expanded village of Kidlington to the left. There have been many as yet unmet demands for a new station here.

Soon we see the Cotswold line from Worcester trailing in to join us at Wolvercote Junction, before we pass under road bridges and run down between the lush pastures of Port Meadow, with the Thames and the wooded Wytham Hill beyond, to our right; and the North Oxford suburbs to our left. At Oxford North Junction is a fairly recent connection to the former L&NWR line from Cambridge, which used to carry a service known as the 'Brains Trains' until 1967; and since May 1987 has been used by an experimental passenger service to Bicester.

Oxford had a wooden station of nineteenth-century vintage until 1972, when modern buildings were opened and these are now subject to further redevelopment. The city of Oxford is described on page 61, and there are good views of its spires and towers as our train continues southwards, crossing the Thames ½ mile south of the station. The line between Didcot and Oxford, over which we are now travelling, was opened in 1844 and the reservoirs that appear shortly on our left are believed to have originated as gravel pits to provide ballast for the line.

We pass under the Oxford bypass, and the former route to Princes Risborough, still used for freight as far as Morris Cowley, diverges and crosses the Thames to our left.

We follow its valley down to Radley – junction for a former branch to the town of Abingdon, whose church tower can be seen away to the right – then cross and recross the river. In between the two crossings is a spur of land on which the rather isolated Culham Station is situated. Another unstaffed halt follows, at Appleford, and then we can see the cooling towers of Didcot power-station ahead.

If we are on a fast train, it will probably now take the Didcot avoiding line, with good views of the Great Western Railway Society's Steam Centre, before heading down through the Goring Gap to Reading and beyond. Local services, and some long-distance ones, draw into Didcot Parkway Station, with connections for Swindon, South Wales, and the West Country.

READING–BASINGSTOKE
by Sue Cooper

The 14-mile line between Reading and Basingstoke has a dual role: it is part of the link from the Midlands to the South Coast used by long-distance passenger and freight trains and it also serves some delightful country on the border of Berkshire and Hampshire.

The expresses from Manchester, Birmingham, and similar places to Southampton, Bournemouth, and Poole, call only at Reading and Basingstoke, at each of which busy stations there is a wide range of other connections. Local trains are frequent – one an hour, even on Sundays – and some of them run through to Portsmouth Harbour. They call at two village stations, Mortimer and Bramley, as well as Reading West.

We leave the mainline to Westbury at Southcote Junction, on the outskirts of Reading and soon pass under the M4 – after which the double-track line climbs gently into undulating country, following the valley of a small stream.

Mortimer is a neat little station 7¼ miles from Reading, built in the Swiss Chalet style found quite often on the old GWR. It serves a straggling village, dominated by a tall church spire, situated on the other side of the stream, among wheatfields and woodlands.

On rising ground to the south of Mortimer was Calleva Atrebatum, one of the principal towns of Roman Britain. It is now Silchester, a small village; and all that remains of the great Roman settlement is its long surrounding wall, enclosing fields in which local farmers have found artefacts that are now in a small museum at the western end. You can walk along part of the wall, near the little twelfth-century church and the shell of the amphitheatre, both of which are well worth visiting.

Do not expect a bus to take you from Mortimer to Silchester; but it is a pleasant walk or cycle ride of some 2 miles along winding country lanes – quiet and relaxing, yet so easily accessible from the busy towns of Reading and Basingstoke, and within quite easy reach of London.

A bicycle would also be handy if you alight at Bramley, the other intermediate station, 3¼ miles farther south; for some 4 miles to the east of it is the great seventeenth-century house of Stratfield Saye. It belonged to the first Duke of Wellington and is worth seeing for its paintings, state coach, and extensive gardens (telephone 0256-882882 for details).

A few more miles through rolling country brings your train back into the busy modern world as you pass down through the curved cutting into Basingstoke Station.

LONDON WATERLOO–SOUTHAMPTON
by Jon Honeysett

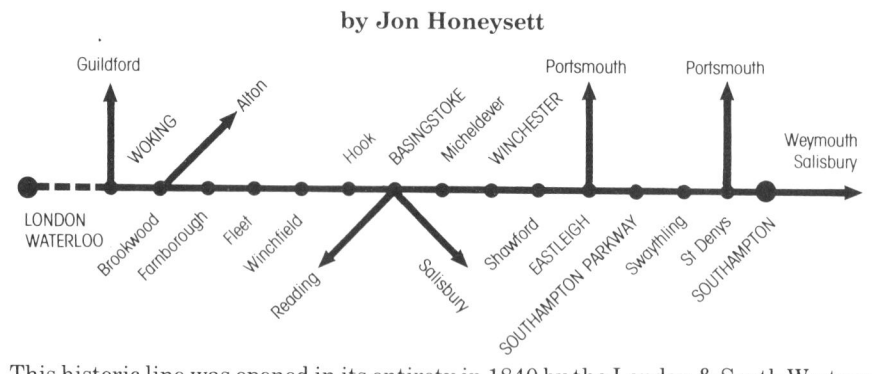

This historic line was opened in its entirety in 1840 by the London & South Western Railway, to link the capital with the port of Southampton. The original London terminus was at Nine Elms, but in 1848 the L&SWR moved to the present site at Waterloo, where the station grew in size until its completion in 1922; though there are plans to enlarge it even further to accommodate trains from Europe, via the Channel Tunnel.

The route to Southampton, designed by civil engineer Joseph Locke, is superbly aligned with the minimum of gradients, and runs through Woking, Basingstoke, Winchester, and Eastleigh to the ancient port at the confluence of the Itchen and Test rivers at the head of Southampton Water. The unique 'double tides' and sheltered anchorage at Southampton were to be exploited by the L&SWR and the Southern Railway, the latter company embarking on a massive scheme in 1927 which expanded the already large docks, to reclaim the Test River mud-flats and turn them into the 'New' or Western Docks, capable of handling the world's largest ships.

By the outbreak of the Second World War, Southampton could justifiably claim to be 'Britain's premier port', for as well as being home to a host of huge liners, the port handled millions of tons of freight, including perishable foodstuffs. The excellent rail configuration ensured ease of access to other parts of the country; while the close proximity of London, just 79 miles to the north-east, meant that passengers could alight at Waterloo within two and a half hours of disembarking. Fresh fruit and vegetables would be carried by fast freight to the Nine Elms refrigerated 'cold store'.

Today, the prosperity of Southampton depends on bulk-container traffic, with only the occasional ocean liner, such as the *Queen Elizabeth 2* and *Canberra* gracing its quays. The docks are operated by Associated British Ports and the site of the former Nine Elms 'cold store' is now the New Covent Garden. Nevertheless, the mainline is still very busy, with Freightliner trains operating from the port's two container terminals, vying with the oil-products trains from the world's sixth largest refinery at Fawley, on the west side of Southampton Water. Conventional freight is handled by Speedlink rail services, though the perishable foodstuffs to New Covent Garden now go by road.

Passenger services have maintained the tradition of speed and comfort along the

'Billiard Table line', as it was known to generations of railwaymen. Where once King Arthur or Merchant Navy Class steam locomotives (many of them built at Eastleigh) sped the expresses and the Ocean Liner boat trains, since 1967 Joseph Locke's railway has been the domain of fast electrics, of four, eight, or twelve cars.

The service frequency for the past twenty years has been three trains an hour in each direction from Waterloo to Southampton and Bournemouth. The hourly fast service takes just seventy minutes to reach Southampton and calls only at Southampton Parkway; while the semi-fast takes ninety-three minutes, calling additionally at Clapham Junction, Woking, Basingstoke, Winchester, and Eastleigh. The local service takes 110 minutes, calling at Surbiton, Woking, then all stations to Southampton and Bournemouth.

From May 1988, the extension of electrification from Branksome (Bournemouth) to Weymouth sees the London–Southampton railway operating the world's fastest third-rail electric multiple units, the five-car Class 442 air-conditioned sets, able to run at 100 m.p.h. The service frequency should remain the same – three trains per hour in each direction – with faster over-all timings. The ten-car fast service will, as now, operate to Weymouth with the leading set only – detaching the trailing set at Poole; the semi-fast will work to Wareham and then terminate; while the local will operate as far as Poole.

Our train speeds through the South London suburbs to Woking, a very busy station handling mainline passenger trains from Waterloo to Portsmouth, Bournemouth, Salisbury, and Exeter, as well as commuter trains from Alton, Aldershot, and Basingstoke. It is also a terminus for the newly introduced shuttle service from Staines; while for airline passengers there is also a dedicated coach link from Woking Station right to the terminals within Heathrow.

Our local electric train for Southampton and Bournemouth is identified by its '93' headcode on the driving cab front, and we must ensure we join the front four-car set; for just as the Southern practice of half a century of providing headcodes is maintained, so, too, is the practice of 'splitting' multiple-unit electric trains. The rear four-car set has its control cables disconnected by a member of the station staff, a driver boards its cab, and it becomes a separate train to Farnham, departing three minutes after us. At thirteen minutes past the hour, our train accelerates briskly away from Woking, with the mainline to Havant and Portsmouth diverging to our left.

The pre-war electrification of the lines from Waterloo to Portsmouth, Alton, and Reading, master-minded by Sir Herbert Walker, greatly increased land values on the Surrey–Hampshire border. 'The pine-clad Southern Electric suburbs' so described by the late Sir John Betjeman, can be glimpsed through the rhododendron shrubs that border the line as we approach Brookwood, our first stop, 3 miles west of Woking. From here, since the turn of the century, vast numbers of soldiers will have alighted for the barracks at Pirbright and the rifle ranges at Bisley, while on the north side of the station can be seen the Basingstoke Canal.

This eighteenth-century canal branches off from the Wey Navigation to Byfleet and volunteer labour has restored its use over considerable lengths. For information, contact the Canal Manager, Ash Lock, Aldershot (telephone 0252–313810), since the company has vessels for hire, including one boat which can accommodate wheelchairs. Visitors to the canal are recommended to alight at Winchfield Station. Though no sign exists of the track today, a line once ran from the south side of Brookwood Station to Necropolis, a huge cemetery built in Victorian times as a final resting-place for Londoners denied burial in a city hard pressed for space.

Our train, passing the flying junction with the Alton line, runs through Deepcut Cutting and a short tunnel, over which is carried the Basingstoke Canal, and crosses over the electric line from Ascot to Ash Vale, singled at this point, followed swiftly by the Blackwater River and the non-electrified double-track line from Wokingham to Ash and Guildford. The small Farnborough North Station can be seen immediately north of our overbridge on that route. With the advent of the Channel Tunnel, it is to be hoped that the full potential of this 'BR outer-orbital route' will be realised, with third-rail electrification all the way from Reading to Tonbridge.

Nine miles west of Woking, we enter Farnborough Main, serving a town of 50,000 people and virtually part of Aldershot to the south. To most of us, the name Farnborough is synonymous with the famous air displays held every two years at the Royal Aircraft Establishment airfield a mile from the station. Dating back to before the First World War, the airfield witnessed the humble beginnings of aviation, with frail flying machines and airship balloons; now the research laboratories deal with advanced jet aircraft, and medical aspects of high altitude and space flight.

From Farnborough to Basingstoke, the mainline is virtually straight, with barely perceptible differences in grade, and for nearly a century has been a 'race-track' – recorded speeds of 100 m.p.h. have been noted behind electric, diesel, and even the last generation of steam locomotives, as drivers took advantage of the clear well-signalled sections ahead of them. Fleet Station, 3 miles west of Farnborough, and situated on the north shore of Fleet Pond, has seen an enormous increase in patronage since electrification in 1967, as property spreads out across the sandy heathlands of north-east Hampshire.

Four miles west is our next stop, Winchfield, which also marks a noticeable change in the scenery – the silver birches, pines, and heathland give way to more arable land – the beginning of the 'Strong Country' and Wessex proper, nicely promoted in the past by the former brewery, Strong of Romsey, in the form of large lineside advertisements depicting Southern steam-hauled trains racing through a mellow landscape. Pleasant country walks commence from Winchfield, with the canal a short distance to the south at Barley Mow Bridge, while farther down the B3016 lies the old town of Odiham, which dates back to Saxon times and holds much of interest to the historian. North of Winchfield lies Yately Common Country Park, once the haunt of highwaymen (telephone 0252–874346).

Hook Station, 2 miles on, also gives access to Odiham and the western end of the Basingstoke Canal at Greywell Tunnel. For walkers, Basing House in the valley of the River Lodden to the west is worth a visit. Open at week-ends, April to September, and daily during June, July, and August, for those interested in the history of the Civil War it is not to be missed (telephone 0256–467294).

Basingstoke, 23 miles west of Woking, is the largest centre of population between London and Southampton and a very important railway junction. The town has grown enormously since the Second World War and now hosts a variety of light industries and commercial office development – the Automobile Association headquarters is based in a skyscraper block visible for miles around. The Willis Museum at the Old Town Hall, Market Place (telephone 0256–465902) has displays of the geology and natural history of the area. (For bus times in the area, including Old Basing, telephone 0256–464501.)

Heading west from Basingstoke we pass over a dual carriageway, and here a branch to Alton curved away to our left; now nothing remains of it except for some earthworks, the line having closed in 1932. The track layout now alters at Worting Junction, with the centre two up and down fast lines changing to non-electrified down and up lines to Salisbury and Exeter and dramatically curving away to our right as they pass under the up electrified line from Southampton to Battledown Flyover.

The country is now typical Downland, with wide views, rolling fields of corn and barley, and huge flocks of sheep on pastures interspersed with clumps of beech trees and copses of hazel. The chalk cuttings provide a natural habitat for a variety of flora and fauna, and as we pass through Litchfield Tunnel, our double-track electric line begins its long descent to Southampton. In steam days this 'summit' of over 300 feet meant a long slog for the fireman on the up line from the coast at sea-level. Passing through two more tunnels at Popham, we emerge into a large area carved out of the chalk, containing sidings and a massive concrete structure on the eastern edge. This is an oil-fuel storage depot, strengthened against the possibility of air attack during the Second World War and still in use today. We have arrived at Micheldever.

This station, some 10 miles south-west of Basingstoke, serves the rather remote hamlets of West Stratton and Micheldever itself, which lies over 2 miles away from it. The platform is of the 'island' type, with down trains stopping on its east side, and up trains on the west. Until 1967, this section was quadrupled, hence the rather substantial station building that stands on what was once a platform.

Pulling away from Micheldever, the train now runs on the top of a long embankment flanked by mature beech trees until the track becomes quadrupled at Wallers Ash. This passing loop was designed to allow the faster passenger trains to overtake the slower-moving freight traffic; these days, however, it sees less use, since most freight trains move at speeds in excess of 60 m.p.h.

We pass through Wallers Ash Tunnel and its long cutting, and suddenly the earth embankment that once carried the single-track line to Alton comes into view on our left. To the right the formation of the former Didcot, Newbury & Southampton Junction Railway can just be glimpsed passing underneath our line.

The city of Winchester, once the Saxon capital of Wessex, comes into view, though briefly, since the station is situated at the north end of a deep cutting. For the tourist there is a great deal to see, not least the Cathedral and the Great Hall, and a day spent in the city is soon gone. For elderly rail travellers to Winchester, it is advisable to leave a spare margin of time to return to the station, as it lies at the top of a hill of some steepness. (For information about the many sights to visit in Winchester, telephone 0962–54411.)

For walkers, the countryside all round is lovely, from the water-meadows alongside the River Itchen to Farley Mount Country Park about 3 miles to the west (telephone 0962–64221 for information about Farley Mount, and for bus services in the area telephone 0962–52352). There are many good-quality hotels and guest-houses in Winchester, for those who consider making the city a base for exploring Wessex.

We have just 13 miles left now to our destination. Emerging from the long cutting, we can see the Iron Age earthworks round the top of St Catherine's Hill to our left that guarded the Itchen Valley from the south, and the long viaduct that carried the DN&SJR to its junction with our mainline at Shawford. This quiet village 3 miles south of Winchester has a pretty walk alongside the waters of the canalised section of the Itchen, easily accessible from the station. The line once more becomes quadrupled and at Allbrook the marshalling yards mark the northern boundary of Eastleigh.

When the L&SWR moved its carriage works from Nine Elms in 1890, and its locomotive works in 1909, to Eastleigh, the prosperity of the town was assured for the next fifty years, and although there are many other industries within the borough, the 'Works' are always known to refer to the railway workshops. Now the 'Works' are refurbishing rolling-stock, and carrying out maintenance overhauls to diesel and electro-diesel locomotives as opposed to building new ones. The carriage works has long since closed, and its adjacent sidings are being removed, but British Rail Engineering Ltd remains a major employer in the town. Just before our train slides into Platform 3, we see on the right the panel signal-box, controlling the multiple-aspect signalling from Worting Junction right down to Bournemouth, and from Cosham to Dean on the cross-country route, of which the Romsey–Eastleigh–Fareham section can be seen entering to the right.

Eastleigh now has its own museum in the High Street, about five minutes' walk from the station, with displays depicting the history of the area from the arrival of the railway in 1840. (For information telephone 0703–643026; and for local bus services telephone 0703-618233.) Track rationalisation, and the closure of the passenger service from Eastleigh to Romsey, has left a rather unsightly up-side station frontage, with a redundant trackless platform. Fortunately a new station, funded jointly by BR and the Council, is to be constructed soon – but sadly, to date, there has been no response to the RDS proposal to reintroduce passenger trains between Eastleigh and Romsey, which would serve the huge population of Chandlers Ford, even though the route is used daily for freight trains and occasionally for passenger trains diverted because of engineering work.

As we leave Eastleigh and pass the BREL works and motive-power depot on our left, we shortly enter Southampton Parkway Station, just 1 mile south. Built in 1966 as Southampton Airport Station, with two simple concrete platforms, unstaffed for most of the day, the station was upgraded in status and provided with a modern booking-office and passenger accommodation in 1986 and renamed Southampton Parkway because of its close proximity to the M27. It has been extremely successful, with the car park already full to capacity to the point where an extension has become necessary. The fact that all trains call there, with Waterloo just sixty-two minutes away by the fast service non-stop, coupled with increased airline flights to the Channel Islands, Paris, and even Amsterdam and Belfast, from the airport just two minutes' walk from its platforms, has ensured its instant popularity.

Less than a mile south is Swaythling Station, in a suburb of Southampton and very convenient for students at the University, whose residential blocks can be seen on the left. From outside the station's up side, approximately four minutes' walk, are bus stops served by CityBus with destinations throughout the city.

A further mile south is our last station, St Denys, where the double-track line from Portsmouth and Fareham curves sharply in from the left. We then run alongside the tidal section of the River Itchen. We have reached the Solent at last, while to our right are the inner suburbs of Southampton, adjacent to the Bevois Valley freight terminal. The mainline swings very sharply to our right under Northam Road Bridge, while the track that runs straight on down to our left is all that remains of the original mainline from London to Southampton Terminus. It is used by the occasional boat train, while the handsome Terminus building, designed by Sir William Tite, and bypassed by the line into the Eastern Docks, has been restored and transformed into a casino and restaurant. Northam actually had its own station on that line, while the remains of track formation of a spur linking the Terminus to the present Southampton Station can just be discerned to our left. Through a brick-lined cutting our train then plunges under the city centre, to emerge in what was known variously as Blechynden, West, Central, and now plain Southampton Station, overlooked by the Civic Centre clock which should read half past the hour – journey's end.

SOUTHAMPTON–POOLE
by Colin Mortimer

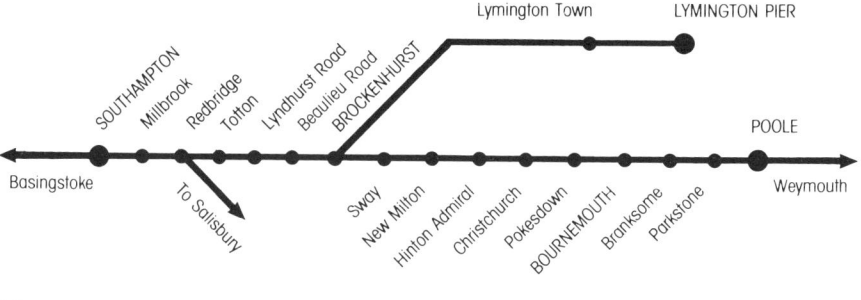

Services from Southampton to Poole are frequent. Monday to Saturday sees three trains an hour to Bournemouth and at least one per hour continuing to Poole and Weymouth. Reduced services operate on a Sunday. In addition to these electric trains, inter-regional diesel services operate from Edinburgh, Glasgow, Newcastle, Liverpool, and Manchester, terminating at Poole except for summer Saturday Holidaymaker Express services which are extended to Weymouth.

The present route did not exist until the 1880s, but many of its component parts date from 1847. In this year, Southampton Tunnel opened, connecting the London & Southampton Railway with the Southampton & Dorchester Railway which ran via Brockenhurst and Ringwood, and, because of its tortuous route, was nicknamed 'Castleman's Corkscrew'. The Lymington branch opened in 1858 and the direct route to Christchurch in 1888. The section thence to Bournemouth opened in stages in the 1870s and 1880s, with the present Bournemouth Station opening in 1888.

Southampton Station has four platforms, plus a bay on the down side for parcels traffic, and possesses all facilities. A refurbishment programme is currently in progress to update the ticket-office and travel centre. The tower office block, Overline House, accommodates the Area Manager for this line. An interesting feature at the London end is the overbridge with its recent maritime flag embellishments.

Our train leaves Southampton Station and immediately on the left the occasional ocean-going liner may be seen. Container ships in the main keep the docks reasonably busy and are the reason why Southampton has two Freightliner terminals.

Before the first station, Millbrook, is the branch to the Western Docks, used less now that GPO parcels traffic has ceased to be carried by rail. As you leave the station, look right for Southampton Freightliner terminal and left for the Maritime Freightliner terminal. Then come the Freightliner wagon repair works followed by

Lymington.

the CM&EE and the CCE works. Redbridge, the next station, is not only used by BR staff but also serves a densely populated area of West Southampton.

The train then has to cross the River Test by a causeway, which is immediately preceded on the right by the line to Romsey, Salisbury, and Bristol branching off to the north. Totton Station serves a very large residential area separated from the city of Southampton by the River Test but linked by the rail causeway and by a modern road bridge which replaced the very narrow stone bridge which can still be seen a stone's throw up river.

Pulling out of Totton Station we see on the left a short spur that goes under the A35, formerly serving Eling Wharf but now truncated for roofing-tile and aggregate traffic only; and then, after the level crossing, reception sidings for this traffic and domestic coal. Then comes the freight line to Marchwood for Ministry of Defence traffic and Fawley for oil traffic.

As we approach Lyndhurst Road Station, the houses give way to open country followed by the village of Ashurst, the nearest populated area to the station.

Lyndhurst itself is some 2½ miles farther west on the A35 and can be reached by bus running at least one per hour from this station or from Brockenhurst. Lyndhurst Road Station is an ideal stopping-off place for a pie and a pint, at the nearby hotel, and for exploring the eastern side of the New Forest.

The train now starts its journey through the forest, with wooded enclosures to the left and heathland to the right. The New Forest ponies seem to enjoy the boggy heathland and it is not uncommon to see their hooves sink in. The train crosses the Beaulieu River, very narrow at this point, before arriving at Beaulieu Road Station – like the previous one, now unstaffed but with a well-appointed hotel next to it where you can have a bite to eat and quench your thirst before setting out on a delightful 4-mile walk across the heath and through the forest to Beaulieu. Before you set off, note the stock-pens on the left where the New Forest pony sales are held during August, September, and October.

On arriving at Beaulieu, you will be rewarded by what this attractive village has to offer. There is the National Motor Museum; Palace House and its gardens, the residence of Lord Montagu; the remains of Beaulieu Abbey and, some 2 miles down the Beaulieu River, Buckler's Hard, a charming and unspoilt eighteenth-century hamlet where ships of the line that fought at Trafalgar were built.

Leaving Beaulieu Road Station with heathland on either side, the train soon enters forested enclosures where, particularly on the right-hand side close to the line, deer can be seen feeding. The line turns westward soon – one of the twists of 'Castleman's Corkscrew' – and then the forest gives way to grassland and the large village of Brockenhurst on the right.

Brockenhurst is a good jumping-off point to explore the beauty of the New Forest. There are many forest walks that allow you to observe the wide variety of trees and wildlife and, of course, the ponies. The Forestry Commission produces leaflets to assist visitors to enjoy the Forest. Brockenhurst itself has a good range of hotels, guesthouses, shops, and eating-places, and is an ideal holiday centre. Lyndhurst, the administrative 'capital' of the New Forest, about 4 miles north, is also a must for the visitor. Among its interesting buildings is the fine seventeenth-century Queen's House from which the forest is administered.

Leaving Brockenhurst's large station with its four through platforms, we see the Lymington branch diverging to the left. Almost immediately look right to see the course of the original route to Bournemouth via Ringwood. Through a cutting surrounded by bracken, heath, and rough grassland, our train arrives at Sway whose station, framed by pine trees, still has its original combination of single-storey ticket-office and gabled house. Delightful walks can be had by alighting here as the western edge of the New Forest is close to the station.

As the train leaves on a short embankment, you have just time to look left and see Sway Tower, a prominent landmark 218 feet high and built by Judge Peterson in 1879. What is interesting about this tower is that he had it built in reinforced concrete to demonstrate the potential of the material for this type of construction, which was in its infancy at the time, and in so doing pioneered the use of shuttering. The tower, a mausoleum for himself, has been referred to as Peterson's Folly. It is out of bounds to the public. A near-continuous cutting follows before we arrive at New Milton Station. Alight here for Barton-on-Sea.

Hinton Admiral is reached through a cutting whose banks at the western end are adorned with primroses in the spring. If you alight here and turn left out of the station yard and over the railway, and then take a short walk to the A35, turning right across it you will find situated left at the crossroads the Cat and Fiddle – a delightful hostelry where you will not be disappointed by the food and drink on offer.

Both New Milton and Hinton Admiral are but a short distance from Christchurch Bay, where cliff walks can be enjoyed at Highcliff and Barton-on-Sea.

For the train it is now downhill all the way to journey's end. On leaving Hinton Admiral, after a short tunnel, the line runs on an embankment with fields on the right, a nearly built-up area on the left, and Christchurch ahead. Braking hard for the tight curves our train crosses the River Avon, whose banks are much frequented by anglers, to arrive at Christchurch. Difficult to see now, but right between the River Avon and the road overbridge before our arrival in Christchurch Station is the course of the old railway to Ringwood, more easily traceable northwards from the old Hurn Station, where the station house and platforms still exist.

Christchurch is best known for its priory, built in the eleventh and early twelfth centuries. Its splendour and beauty can only be appreciated by a visit. Other places of interest in this delightful town include the Quay, the well-kept gardens, the river walk to the Quay and close by Mudeford and Hengistbury Head. Opportunities for sailing and fishing abound and there is a modern shopping centre.

An urban area now extends all the way to Poole. The River Stour is crossed and, like the Avon, it flows into Christchurch Harbour. Pokesdown, the next station, used to enjoy four tracks but is now reduced to two. Alight here for Boscombe and Southbourne. Both are within walking distance, but if you prefer a bus, these run frequently. Boscombe has a pier and there are cliff walks towards both Southbourne and Bournemouth with magnificent views of Poole Bay.

Our train soon passes the site of Boscombe Station – the only closed station on this line – and just before we run into Bournemouth Station, on the left, there used to be inclined sidings to a freight depot, whose site is now occupied by a DIY store.

Bournemouth Station has up and down platforms and a bay on the up side for stopping services; but the extra tracks in the middle were removed with the introduction of electrification. Although the station has all the facilities, it is hoped that a bright new station will appear in the very near future, as the existing Late Victorian structure does not blend into the current image of Bournemouth with its modern shopping facilities, theatres, cinemas, conference centre, and high-rise business premises.

Bournemouth is a high-class resort with a mild climate, sandy beaches, beautiful parks and public gardens, coastal views, amusement pier – in fact everything that a holiday-maker would wish for. The Tourist Information Bureau is situated in Westover Road, opposite Bournemouth Gardens (telephone 0202–291715).

Most trains continue westwards from Bournemouth. Just before the next station, Branksome, look left to see a beautiful brick-arched viaduct that used to provide access to Bournemouth West Station. Sadly it is not now used and consequently vegetation has taken over completely. Although the West Station is now obliterated and the lines truncated, to enable the Bournemouth centre bypass to be built, the remains of this branch still serve the carriage sidings and depot, which has recently been extended to cater for the new stock entering service in 1988.

Branksome Station is currently being refurbished. Before the boundary changes, the station sign advised travellers to alight here for East Dorset; nowadays it serves West Bournemouth and Canford Cliffs.

The next station, Parkstone, serves East Poole and Sandbanks which, as its name suggests, has a fine stretch of sand. For the more adventurous, catch the ferry to cross the mouth of Poole Harbour from Sandbanks to Studland. If you check bus times, you may find that you are also able to take in the beautiful scenery of the Isle of Purbeck and rejoin a train at Wareham. The ferry takes bicycles, thus offering greater facility for exploring the area around Poole's great natural harbour.

We catch our first glimpse of this harbour shortly after our train leaves Parkstone and we cross Parkstone Bay via a causeway with a delightful boating-lake on the right bounded by Poole Park with its many attractions – miniature golf, miniature railway, wildfowl lake, zoo, bowling green, tennis-courts, and not forgetting a cafeteria and restaurant overlooking the lakes.

After negotiating a barrier crossing through the town's main thoroughfare, which is pedestrianised, and a very tight curve, we reach Poole Station, which is currently being rebuilt. The end product will be a much larger station in a 'grand marquee' style featuring four dark blue steel masts supporting by cables a silver-coloured barrel-vaulted roof enclosing 500 square feet, with all the usual amenities.

Poole has much to offer the holiday-maker. Its harbour is the largest natural one in the world and attracts a variety of traffic from the Continent, including steel which goes inland by rail on the freight-only line from Hamworthy goods to Hamworthy Station, 2¾ miles farther west. From the quay, pleasure-boats will take you on a trip round the harbour or ferry you to Sandbanks, Wareham, Swanage, or Brownsea Island. The last is a must, where you will find unspoilt beauty, secluded beaches, heathland, woodland, and wildlife such as silka deer and red squirrels.

The old town is steeped in history and among the many places of interest is Poole Pottery where you will be most welcome to take a conducted tour. In complete contrast is the modern part of Poole where in the Arndale Centre, only minutes from the station, you will find the most up-to-date stores and shops all under cover. Indoor sports facilities are to be found under the same roof and opposite, via a subway, is Poole Arts Centre which provides a wide range of shows, both theatre and film.

The Poole Tourism Centre, Poole Quay, Poole, Dorset, BE15 1HE (telephone 0202–673322) will provide you with all information; and there is also an information kiosk in the Arndale Centre. The train journey farther west into Dorset is described in our companion volume, *South West by Rail*.

BASINGSTOKE–SALISBURY
by Norman Cox

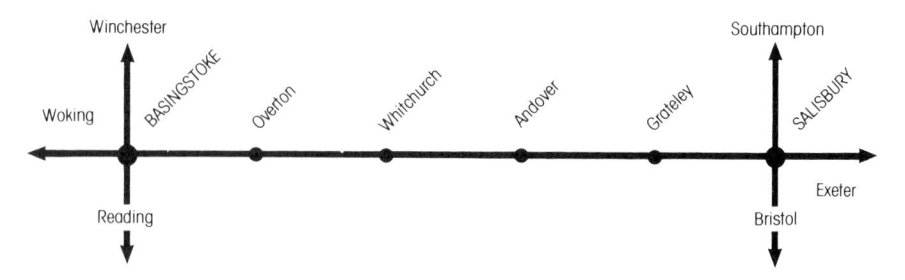

This line is part of the former London & South Western Railway's route to the West Country, with a two-hourly semi-fast Waterloo–Exeter service plus trains which terminate at Salisbury or Yeovil giving a roughly hourly service on the section covered in this article. Not all trains stop at the smaller stations.

We leave the recently refurbished Basingstoke Station in company with the main Southampton and Weymouth electrified lines. Watch out soon for a collection of old station nameboards from all over the United Kingdom in the garden of a lineside house on the right.

Our line separates from the main Southampton one about 3 miles west of Basingstoke at Worting Junction where we bear right under the impressive Battledown Flyover, a steel-girder bridge carrying the up Southampton line over ours.

The first station we come to is Overton, an unmanned halt about ½ mile from the village which is straight down the road to the south. Overton has the infant Test flowing through it from its source about 1½ miles to the east. The old village was to the north of the river – hence the position of the church – but in about 1200 the Bishop of Winchester promoted a new 'planned town' to the south of it.

The village today is rather spoiled by the volume of east–west traffic passing along one of its narrow main streets. However, do not miss the other main street leading southwards, Winchester Street – quiet, wide, and with pleasant shops and houses. This was probably the venue of the sheep fairs when sheep and their wool constituted the main industry of the area.

The church, a fine building with its neat dumpy steeple and chiming tower clock, is entered by an unusual and ancient centre-hinged door, and its oldest architectural feature is its Norman nave pillars. A unique feature in the oak inner porch is a pair of watermark portraits – one of the Queen at her coronation and the other of the Prince of Wales. These were made at the local banknote-paper mill and can be seen when the floodlights behind them are switched on.

A paper-mill was first established in 1719 at Laverstoke, 1½ miles to the west, by Henri Portal, a refugee from France. He found the chalk-stream water of the Test ideal for paper-making. From 1724 to 1950, banknote paper was made here; now it is made at the new mill in Overton. Not only is our own banknote paper manufactured here, but also that for many overseas governments.

Leaving Overton Station to continue our journey, we soon have a fine vista to the south, down the fields, of Overton Church with the village spread out behind it.

Our next station is Whitchurch, on the northern outskirts of this small town on the River Test. Whitchurch is on the old London–Exeter coaching route and the White Hart at the bottom of the hill is one of the old coaching inns.

Carrying straight on to the river bridges we find Whitchurch silk-mill, one of the most interesting features of the town, still weaving silk for specialist uses – including barristers' silks. It is now being restored from a state of near dereliction and parts of the mill are to be open to visitors. An exhibition and shop area are already open at the time of writing. There is a pleasant riverside walk of about ¾ mile westwards from the mill towards the village of Tufton with its small Norman church.

As our train leaves, the trackbed of the old Didcot, Newbury & Southampton Railway can be seen below, particularly on the left. The line passed under ours and had its own station to the west of the town. Passenger traffic ceased in 1962 but it continued to be used by oil trains from Fawley refinery until 1964.

Just over 2 miles farther on we come to the splendid nine-arch St Mary Bourne Viaduct – overlooking on the right extensive watercress-beds. As we leave the viaduct, a careful watch shows where the old Hurstbourne & Fullerton line curved off to the left under a brick overbridge. This line, too, closed under the Beeching Plan in 1964.

Andover Station is approached through the industrial and housing estates which are part of the considerable expansion of the town under the 1960s London overspill scheme, transforming it from a rather sleepy and in parts at least down-at-heel country town, to its present much-improved state with a modern shopping area, technical college and sports complex, and pleasantly landscaped riverside and other areas. The town is dominated architecturally by the parish church – St Mary's – which stands at the highest point, clearly visible on the skyline as we run into the station along the embankment.

Andover Station and environs have recently been altered and refurbished under a joint scheme with TSB Trust Ltd, who have extensive office and training premises in the town, and the Borough and County Councils. Tourist information leaflets are usually available at the station. The town centre can be reached by bus (half-hourly service from the stop outside the station, not the stop opposite) or a ten-minute walk via Bishops Way, Junction Road, and a footpath to the left through an underpass and over the river to the college and sports complex, beyond which is the town centre and bus station.

There is a Tourist Information caravan near this area in the car park by the Town Mill during the tourist season. The Town Mill itself has recently been restored. It is in a pleasant riverside setting and is to be used as a country pub. Other historic buildings are the Angel Inn of 1443 in Upper High Street, Andover's oldest building, the United Reformed Church of 1700 in East Street, the Pollen Almshouses in Marlborough Street, and a number of old houses and shops in Chantry Street. There is also the Norman Gate arch in Upper High Street. Apart from the Town Mill, all these are in the general area of the parish church, St Mary's, at the top of the town.

In Church Close is the Andover Museum – which also incorporates the Museum of the Iron Age, a very imaginative and informative display using artefacts and information from the local Iron Age fortress of Danebury Ring to give an insight into the daily lives and activities of that community. (The museum is open 10 a.m. to 5 p.m. from Tuesday to Saturday and admission is free. Additionally, the Museum of the Iron Age opens 2 to 5 p.m. on Sundays from April to October, and there is a small charge.)

Danebury Ring itself is about 6 miles south-west of Andover – within easy cycling distance but unfortunately not close to public transport. If you do not mind a 2-mile walk, you can take the No. 277 bus (Salisbury or Broughton) from the bus station, alight at the army air camp stop, walk back a bit and go up the lane southwards at the edge of the camp. Bus times are rather intermittent, so enquire at the Hampshire Bus office in West Street, where you can buy 'go anywhere' Explorer day tickets.

Leaving Andover, the third track on the right is the line to army depots at Ludgershall and Tidworth and curves off soon at Red Post Junction. This stub of the old Midland & South Western Junction Railway has recently seen use by steam specials in connection with various local rail events and is a remarkably smooth line to travel.

Continuing westward, we cross the five-arch viaduct over the Pillhill Brook with again extensive watercress-beds – this time on our left. In another 4 miles we arrive at Grateley, an unstaffed halt that has seen busier days, especially when it was junction for Bulford.

Do not be misled into thinking that the hotch-potch of residential and industrial development round the station is Grateley. This area is known as Grateley Station. The village itself lies ¾ mile away to the north-east. With its squat grey-towered church, dating from the twelfth century, it is visible looking back from the station. One item of interest in the church is some medieval stained glass rescued from Salisbury Cathedral when thrown out by the restorer Wyatt in 1787.

Overlooking the whole area is Quarley Hill with its Iron Age fortress – possibly the place where the Council of AD 925 met, called by King Athelstan, to enact the first code of laws to cover all England.

From Grateley Station it is a pleasant cycle ride down the valley through Over, Middle, and Nether Wallop – yes, those are real places – to Dunbridge or Romsey on the Southampton–Salisbury line. About 2½ miles beyond Grateley we come to the site of Bulford Junction where the trackbed of the old railway to Amesbury, closed in 1963, runs off to the north-west, with substantial chalk earthworks.

The prominent building 2 miles farther on to the left is Porton Down experimental station. Porton itself, one mile farther on, recently saw moves by villagers in this growing community to reopen the station – but even as a survey was being made, the bulk of the land was sold for industrial use. There are still hopes for a reopening, but although enough space remains for a platform there is none for convenient parking.

We cross the little Bourne River as it flows to join the Hampshire Avon at Salisbury, and soon come to Laverstock North Junction, where a loop curves off to join the Salisbury–Southampton line. As that line joins ours at Salisbury Tunnel Junction, we immediately enter Fisherton Tunnel and then run into Salisbury with the spire of the Cathedral dominating the skyline to the left.

Salisbury Cathedral.

LONDON WATERLOO–PORTSMOUTH
by Ken Wright

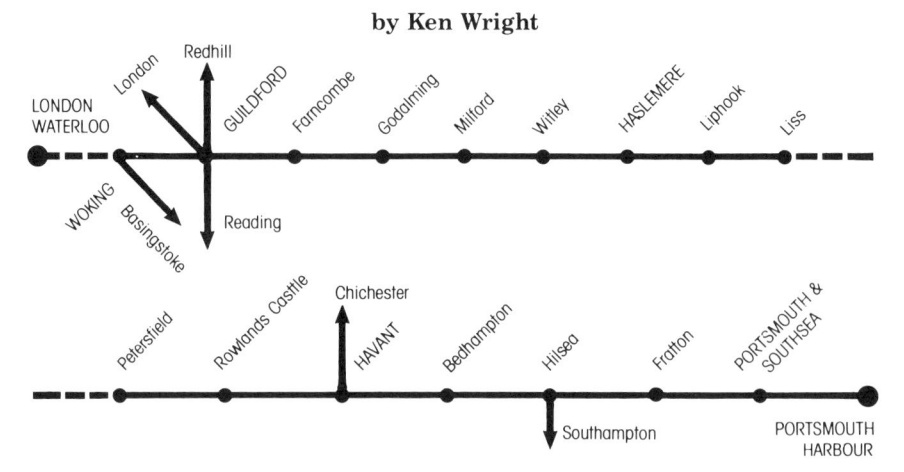

The direct route to Portsmouth was a relatively late addition to the Victorian mainline network, not being completed until 1859 and the harbour extension not until October 1879.

Portsmouth is well served by trains from the capital via this route, with three per hour in each direction, fast, semi-fast, and stopping. Stopping services these days terminate at Surbiton, where there are frequent trains to Waterloo. Guildford provides interchange between the fast and stopping services in both up and down directions for those using the lesser stations on the line and wishing to shorten their travelling times. The best scenery lies between Guildford and Havant since the line has to traverse between these two points both the North and South Downs.

Waterloo is the London terminus for Portsmouth, Southampton, Salisbury, and Exeter. The present station was completed in 1922 and gives to me the most pleasing impressions of space and light which must have been a guiding influence for its designer, J. W. Jacomb-Hood. He travelled to the USA to gather information on station design and this influence shows. The concourse is bright and cheerful with a vast array of shops and restaurants as well as a large travel centre and reservation/booking centre.

The journey out of this grand terminus is on a viaduct with views of the Houses of Parliament, Lambeth Palace, the Tate Gallery, New Covent Garden, and Battersea power-station. Clapham Junction, surely the 'Spaghetti Junction' of the railway network, provides a wide range of connections; after which our train speeds onwards through Wimbledon and into the outer suburbs, with an increasing amount of greenery from playing-fields, parks, and the more spacious back gardens.

We pass through Surbiton the junction for Hampton Court and Esher with Sandown Park Racecourse clearly visible on the left, Weybridge, and Byfleet, before slowing for Woking, where all Portsmouth trains stop before veering south to Guildford.

Through Surrey heathland, interspersed with small thickets, we approach Guildford, with its imposing modern Anglican cathedral on the right. After this important junction with cross-country routes, our train heads south, bisecting the North Downs and following the Wey Valley to Godalming. The long climb to Haslemere now commences, through Wealden country to one of the highest points on Network South East. Between Witley and Haslemere in particular the landscape is densely wooded and in autumn there is a vast splash of differing colours from the mix of conifers and deciduous woodland.

All scheduled services stop at Haslemere, situated in one of the most beautiful parts of the Surrey countryside. The town is known for its late summer Music Festival, in addition to its outstanding natural surroundings. From the station it is a pleasant and not too demanding walk up to Gibbet Hill and the Devil's Punchbowl — which lived up to its name throughout the Middle Ages and beyond as a favourite haunt of highwaymen and footpads on the London–Portsmouth road.

The line descends towards Liphook and Liss, where it crosses the border into Hampshire and follows briefly the course of the River Rother until just before entering Petersfield. Until recently fast services did not stop here so, even in the days of steam, up to 1937 when the whole route was electrified, down services used to attain very high speeds through Petersfield.

Petersfield is a rather pleasant market town, although on the debit side the main A3 Portsmouth road runs through it. One point of interest for the traveller is the rather odd statue of William III (William of Orange). Here we have the famous Dutchman astride an overweight steed with its tail, believe it or not, tied up in a bow. To complete the absurdity, William is dressed in attire which more resembles an outfit worn by a Roman legionary at the time of Augustus rather than that of a gentleman of the late seventeenth century.

Apparently also in the late seventeenth century none other than Samuel Pepys used to stop over at Petersfield on his way to Portsmouth, highwaymen notwithstanding. Indeed, Pepys and his contemporaries had a penchant for living the good life on their stays here and even indulging in the playing of 'bowles' with their wives, whatever that means precisely.

It is also feasible at Petersfield to catch a bus to Selborne — well worth the trip since it was once the home of the renowned naturalist Gilbert White who here wrote his celebrated book *The Natural History and Antiquities of Selborne*, published in 1789. His former residence, The Wales, now houses a memorial library as well as being a museum dedicated to both White and Captain Oates of Antarctic fame.

After leaving Petersfield, the line goes under the main A3 road past some thickly wooded terrain on the right with the northern side of the South Downs now looming into view. Near here is the viewpoint of Buster Hill, one of the high points of the Downs. We plunge through the short Buriton Tunnel of 485 yards before emerging into a fold in the Downs with the steeper ground to the right.

By the time we reach the small stopping services only station of Rowlands Castle, the hills are disappearing from view behind us and we approach the coastal plain on the right-hand curve. The coastal line built by the former London, Brighton & South Coast Railway Company comes in from the left just before we reach Havant Station. This junction was the scene of the infamous 'Battle of Havant' where navvies from both the London & South Western Railway (builders of the line over which we have travelled) and the Brighton company staged a pitched battle using their tools as weapons after the LB&SCR padlocked a locomotive to the points in an attempt to stop the L&SWR from reaching Havant.

Havant has become something of an industrial sprawl on both sides of the track, but it is surely better to see a place alive than in despair and dereliction as some of our northern cities. Havant Station was, until 1963, the junction for trains on the branch to Hayling Island. The island still attracts tourists to its beaches and holiday camps and a regular bus service terminates in the station forecourt.

We now pass through the minor station of Bedhampton and then underneath the concrete viaduct supporting the recently built A3 motorway. It is difficult to discern where exactly Havant ends and Portsmouth begins as it is now built up all the way.

With Farlington Marshes to our left we approach the triangular junction with the line to Southampton veering off to the right. After crossing the creek at the northern end of Portsea Island we pass through Hilsea Station with Portsmouth Rugby Club on the right opposite the gasworks on the left. In former years the aroma here was somewhat pungent, though there was the compensation of seeing a rather splendid shunting locomotive in the sidings.

Past terraced houses and a cemetery we come to Fratton, the extensive sidings and depot containing a motley mixture of rolling-stock. Beyond can be seen the floodlights of Fratton Park, home of Portsmouth Football Club, now after many years back in the First Division where in the past they have won both League and Cup.

After Fratton we shortly enter Portsmouth and Southsea Station, which serves the modern centre. For a town of comparable size to Brighton, the station is disappointing to say the least. Some of the low-level terminal platforms are now disused, since most services now run up the steep ramp to the high level through tracks to the harbour. At the time of writing, some work is being done in the booking-office and concourse areas, and to refurbish the structure above the long island platform on the elevated twin tracks. It was created little better than a gloomy cattle shed, with emphasis on the word 'gloomy', and it gave an impression of having been assembled quickly and cheaply. During the war, the glass was blown out of the outer wall and replaced by a corrugated fabric.

Portsmouth and Southsea Station is within easy walking distance of the modern shopping centre, to your right as you come out of the main entrance opposite the Guildhall. Buses run in the opposite direction to the shingle beach at Southsea where there are the usual seaside entertainments and fun-fair at Clarence Pier.

We move on slowly towards the end of the line at Portsmouth Harbour. In case anyone was in any doubt that Portsmouth was a naval stronghold, here is proof galore. On the left is the United Services Portsmouth sports ground where the cranes and superstructures of the dockyards loom on the horizon. After swinging to the right and then left, we enter Portsmouth Harbour Station.

This is an unusual station in that it is built mostly over the sea. That, of course, is good news for the rail traveller who wishes to continue to Gosport or more commonly for rail passengers to the Isle of Wight by ferry. You literally walk off the train across the short concourse and down the gangway if you wish to proceed farther

Portsmouth Harbour. (*Photo:* Harold Atkinson)

towards Ryde Pier Head. Formerly the ferries were operated by British Rail, but even in private hands they remain integrated with the fast services to and from London.

Details concerning the Isle of Wight can be found on page 57 while the city of Portsmouth is described on page 60.

PORTSMOUTH–WESTBURY
by Jon Honeysett

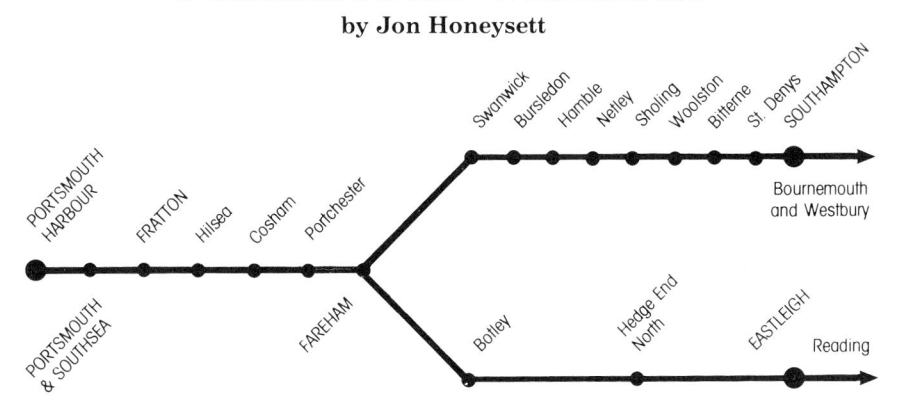

The line from Portsmouth to Salisbury – first via Eastleigh and then additionally via Southampton – did not exist in the true sense until 1889. The first link was a single-track branch line from Bishopstoke (the former name for Eastleigh) to Gosport, on the western edge of Portsmouth Harbour, completed in 1841. Owing to the difficulties encountered with the 'blue clay' terrain between Botley and Fareham, which were to plague the engineers for the next century, the line was closed temporarily, and reopened in 1842. In 1847, the London & South Western Railway pushed west from Eastleigh, to Romsey and Salisbury.

In 1848 a 'branch of a branch' was built by the L&SWR from Fareham to Cosham, with a spur on to Portcreek Junction for Portsmouth, and to Farlington Junction for direct access to the London Brighton & South Coast Railway route from Portsmouth to Havant and Brighton. In 1865, the L&SWR constructed its route from Redbridge, west of Southampton, up the valley of the River Test to Romsey. All that remained to be built was the route from St Denys to Fareham, but by the following year in 1866, the railway had only reached Netley, and that primarily to serve the massive Royal Victoria Hospital, which with the line running right into its grounds had its own station. Not until 1889 did the line from Netley finally link up at Fareham to complete the through route from Portsmouth to Southampton.

In July 1896, the first through passenger train service commenced from Portsmouth to Bristol, running via Fareham, Southampton, Romsey, Salisbury, Westbury, and Bath, with a change of locomotive – from L&SWR to GWR – taking place at Salisbury, a practice maintained right up to the demise of steam traction in 1967.

These through services have, since 1967, had a somewhat chequered history. Dieselisation brought into service Western Region diesel-hydraulic Hymek locomotives heading six-car sets of BR Mark 1 carriages including a buffet car, with usually four trains each way. These gave way to Western Region corridor diesel units, but in the early 1970s the service reached its lowest ebb with non-corridor Hampshire three-car diesel units operating a very basic service from Portsmouth to Bristol approximately every two hours.

Public dissatisfaction made itself felt, and eventually the diesel units were replaced by five-car sets of corridor stock, hauled by Class 31 and then Class 33 diesel locomotives, at hourly intervals throughout the day. British Rail hope to introduce superior rolling-stock on this service by 1990, in the shape of Class 155 Super Sprinter diesel units in multiple, forming four-car sets, operating from Portsmouth Harbour to Bristol and Cardiff. It is hoped to reduce the present fastest timing for the 141-mile route to an even three hours — some achievement compared to steam's fastest timings in 1960 of five hours.

If the future of the Portsmouth–Bristol–Cardiff services depends on the introduction of Super Sprinters, the actual lines's future, at least from St Denys to Portcreek and Farlington Junctions, and Eastleigh to Fareham, is very much dependent on third-rail electrification of these routes. From Redbridge to Salisbury, and from Eastleigh to Romsey, the lines pass through a more rural area, unlikely to be considered for electrification in the foreseeable future, though in the interim the RDS believes there is a case for a diesel service to be reintroduced between Eastleigh and Romsey, reopening the closed station at Chandlers Ford, which now has a growing population already in excess of 20,000.

The 'local' passenger services from Southampton and Eastleigh to Portsmouth are operated by three-car Hampshire diesel units, built in 1957 and intended merely as stop-gaps for ten to fifteen years, to be replaced by electric units. The Hampshires are non-corridor, and their motors are unable to move the trains at anything like the speed needed to compete effectively with the private car or the bus services that ply the M27 linking Southampton and Eastleigh to Portsmouth and Havant. Non-corridor stock means considerable fare evasion, particularly from unstaffed stations between Portsmouth and Southampton. The main lines at either end were electrified in 1937 and 1967 respectively, and have consequently seen a rise in traffic; the non-electrified lines have, by contrast, seen patronage stagnate and even decline.

In 1987, British Rail, supported by Hampshire County Council and other bodies, including RDS, submitted fresh plans to the Department of Transport to electrify these lines. Approval was finally given in April 1988, and so by the time you are reading this book, work should be under way. BR will then have the chance to compete more effectively with the roads for local traffic; and opportunities will open up for through services from Southampton to Gatwick Airport and London Bridge; and from Fareham to Waterloo via Eastleigh.

So much for the future. What of these lines themselves? For the Portsmouth–Westbury route, let me suggest using the hourly service from Portsmouth Harbour to Bristol, mainly because of the comfort of the corridor carriages and their wider windows. To alight at the smaller stations will necessitate using the slower non-corridor diesel units. Let us hope that by the time you, dear reader, venture along the line, it will be in a brand-new electric train!

The through trains to Bristol and Cardiff all start from Portsmouth Harbour Station, giving advertised connections to the ships and to the ferries from the Isle of Wight. If possible, find a seat facing the locomotive, on the left-hand side. At ten minutes past each hour, the train will depart and is soon rumbling along the embankment to Portsmouth and Southsea high-level station. A short pause to pick up passengers, and away we go, up through the densely packed suburbs of Portsmouth island. The train slows to cross the tidal 'moats' near the northern defence ramparts of the city and swings sharply to our left at Portcreek Junction.

Cosham Station is situated in the centre of this bustling northern suburb of Portsmouth and immediately behind the Queen Alexandra Hospital rises the bulk of Portsdown Hill. Buses from the station running north to Waterlooville will take you nearly to the top of Portsdown Hill from which, on a clear day, you will be rewarded with spectacular views of the whole of the Solent area — with Portsmouth appearing in miniature, its warships and ferries looking like tiny models, and the north coast of the Isle of Wight providing a most suitable backdrop. The rim of Portsdown Hill is studded with massive brick-built fortifications, dating back to Napoleonic times, and a number of more modern structures serving the electronic needs of the Royal Navy.

Cosham, 5½ miles out, is an important station on the route, even more so now that the huge IBM complex has been built on reclaimed land just to the south, and all the Bristol and Cardiff trains stop here. Some 2½ miles on, our train passes through Portchester, the famous castle of that name being glimpsed to the south. Dating back to pre-Roman times, the castle was recognised as a perfect anchorage by the Romans who built the outer walls, and by the Saxons who maintained it, but it was the Normans who constructed the keep in the twelfth century in the reign of Henry II. From here, Henry V set sail for Agincourt, and later Henry VIII and Anne Boleyn went hunting in the countryside to the north, to Southwick.

The later Southwick House, on the other side of Portsdown Hill, on 6 June 1944 was the nerve-centre for the greatest maritime invasion in history – 'Operation Overlord' – when every creek and river-mouth in the Solent and Southampton Water, was crammed with landing-craft and soldiers. Portchester Castle is about ¾ mile south of the station, while close by is Fort Nelson, one of the aforementioned Napoleonic forts, now open to the public. (For information telephone 0329–233734.)

The whole coastal belt, from Emsworth through to Redbridge, has since 1945 become a vast agglomeration of housing and light industry, with actual areas of open country becoming few and far between. As the train crosses the long viaduct to enter Fareham, 11 miles from Portsmouth, the density of road traffic on the A27 alongside bears witness to the highest degree of car-ownership in the United Kingdom. The growth of huge American-style 'shopping marts' along the A27 and M27 'corridor' has serious implications for the future prosperity of the traditional shopping centres of Portsmouth, Fareham, and Southampton, and indeed for local public transport – unless bus services can be integrated with trains as 'feeders' to upgraded park-and-ride stations.

A sharp curve to the right brings us to a stop in Fareham Station, the long straight line coming in from our left being the truncated remains of the former route to Gosport, now a freight-only line to the Royal Navy depot sidings at Bedenham, some 3 miles to the south. Fareham town centre is some ten minutes' walk from the station, with buses serving the large suburbs and Stubbington, Lee-on-the-Solent, and Gosport available there. (For bus information telephone 0329–234373 or 232208.)

As we pull away from Fareham, the single-track line to Botley and Eastleigh diverges to our right and enters a tunnel, while our train begins to tackle the sinuous course of the route to St Denys – 12 miles of steep gradients and sharp curves with no fewer than seven stations *en route*, three of which are unstaffed and four partially manned. We cross the lower end of the Meon Valley, and from the bridge over the river, through the trees, can see Titchfield Abbey, where Henry VI married Margaret of Anjou. The building was later converted to a stately house and in the seventeenth century Charles I fled there, only to be captured and sent to Carisbrooke Castle on the Isle of Wight. The little town can be reached quite easily by bus from Fareham or our next station, Swanwick, 4 miles to the west. Visitors to the yachting centre at Warsash should alight at Swanwick and catch a bus on the nearby A27.

Descending the bank, our train passes at speed through Swanwick, with the M27 alongside, then slows for the left-hand curve across the River Hamble, over Bursledon Bridge. When the tide is high, and the sun is shining, a picture-postcard view is seen of 'Tarrant' the fictitious BBC television location featured in *Howard's Way*, in reality Old Bursledon, known to millions of viewers as the boatyard, with the old pub, The

Jolly Sailor, nestling by the river-bank. Just as land values have rocketed in South Hampshire, so here mooring space is at a premium and the river is a mass of marina complexes, some with yacht-repair yards attached. Indeed, it is estimated that there are approximately £1 billion's worth of vessels on the Hamble.

Though our train speeds through Bursledon, for the rambler who alights here from an all-stations diesel unit, a very pleasant walk can be had along the west bank of the river, right up to Botley, through the Upper Hamble Country Park and the Hampshire Farm Museum. (For information on these two attractions, telephone the Country Park on 0703–455157 and the Farm Museum on 04892–87055 – they both are open all the year round.)

Our train now climbs a stiff gradient, with some fine views down to the mouth of the river, before entering a cutting and sliding quickly through Hamble Station. Though Hamble is a yachting paradise, it was also famous for its aircraft factories, only one of which now remains – British Aerospace, formerly Hawker Siddeley, and before that Follands. From these hangars emerged the famous Gnat of Red Arrows fame, the Harrier, and generations of civil and military aircraft.

Within two minutes, our locomotive is accelerating up through Netley, a handsome station building, recently renovated, from which a footpath leads alongside the former rail connection into what is now the Royal Victoria Country Park. The hospital, which treated wounded soldiers from the Crimean War to the Second World War, was demolished, leaving just the chapel whose dome can be seen across the tree-tops. The chapel is now the Royal Victoria Centre, and a climb up to the viewing gallery gives fine views across Southampton Water. The grounds, which slope gently down to the shore, now stage numerous events during the year, including vintage vehicle rallies (for information telephone 0703–455157).

Our train soon slows again and passes through Sholing, then Woolston, where on the north side of the new Itchen Bridge, just a few yards from your seat, was the factory, the birthplace of the Supermarine Spitfire, bombed out by the Luftwaffe in 1940. Descending down to sea-level, our train follows the curve of the River Itchen with its wharves and jetties, through the suburb of Bitterne, across the river itself, round the tight curve into and through St Denys Junction.

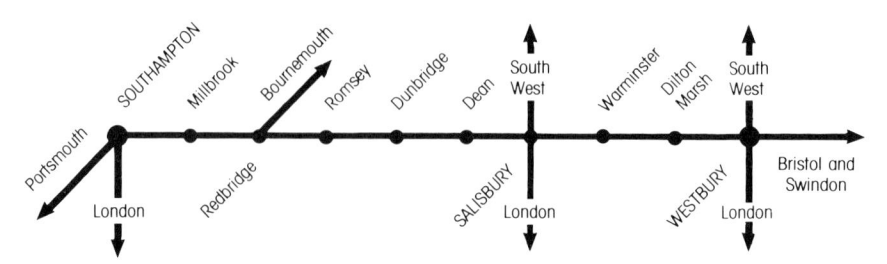

The city of Southampton and the mainline through it are described on pages 60 and 16. We commence the second stage of our journey out past the Western Docks to Redbridge, where we part company with the electrified line to Bournemouth and our train gathers speed as it follows the reed-fringed course of the Test, until some eight minutes later, we slow for the left-hand curve into Romsey.

This compact market town owes its existence to the founding of the Abbey in 907. It was burnt down by the Danes in 994 but was rebuilt and flourished until the Black Death. At the Dissolution it was said to be worth £528. The town gradually recovered, and as our train stops here, it is well worth a visit, with its lovely park just behind the massive Abbey, surrounded by the clear waters of the Test, and a lock over which the salmon leap in season. Some ten minutes' walk south of the town is Broadlands, for many years the home of Lord Mountbatten, and containing many fine mementoes of his service to the nation (for information telephone 0794–516878).

Accelerating away from Romsey, our train passes through the best scenery on the route, with rolling hills to the north marking the Test Valley to Stockbridge and Andover, and shortly before we speed through Dunbridge, the abandoned formation of the line to Andover – nicknamed the 'Sprat & Winkle line' and closed in 1964 – can be seen diverging to the right at the site of what was Kimbridge Junction.

Mottisfont Priory, a National Trust property, is just a mile north-east of Dunbridge Station which, like the next little station, Dean, is ideal for long walks or cycle rides into the heart of Wessex. Cyclists can traverse the 'old gold route' – the B3084 – said to be the route by which the Phoenicians made their way from the coast to the interior.

Some 3 miles west of Dean we see the A36 dual carriageway on our left, partly built on the track formation of the old single-track line to West Moors, closed by Beeching in 1964. Soon our train slows as the magnificent spire of Salisbury Cathedral comes into view, and shortly after we curve sharply to the right, passing the former divergence to the old terminus at Milford. For about a mile we head north, then swing sharply left to join the mainline from Waterloo at Tunnel Junction. A triangular junction was reinstated here in 1981 to allow heavy container trains from Southampton, and passenger trains from Waterloo to Weymouth, to be diverted via Salisbury, without needing to reverse, when the Southampton–Basingstoke route is closed for engineering work. It has also been used as a 'turning triangle' for steam locomotives operating excursions from Salisbury to Yeovil Junction.

We emerge from the tunnel and, a minute or so later, come to a stop in Salisbury Station, conveniently sited for the old part of the city where the great thirteenth-century cathedral – whose spire at 404 feet is the highest in England – is a must for the visitor. Fisherton Street leads into the city centre from the station, and there is an information office here (telephone 0722–27676) or at No. 10 Endless Street (telephone 0722–4956), where you can also find out more about the places of interest in the surrounding area. These include Old Sarum and Stonehenge to the north, to which bus and coach tours are available in summer.

The rail routes to Exeter and Westbury are described in detail in our companion volume, *South West by Rail*. Our cross-country train takes the latter route, built by the Great Western Railway and branching off from the Exeter line at Wilton. It runs along the lovely valley of the River Wyelye, through chalk uplands dotted with tumuli and fortifications dating back to the Stone Age. Five intermediate stations on this route were closed thirty years ago and the run is a fast one, with the 20 miles from Salisbury to Warminster reeled off in twenty-three minutes.

The uplands of Salisbury Plain have been used as the British Army's main training-ground since the Boer War. Indeed, there are species of butterfly, moth, bird, and flowering plant that owe their very existence to the 'machinery of war' which, when the wind is in the right direction, can be heard booming from the artillery ranges at Larkhill and the tank training-grounds at Tilshead.

Our approach to Warminster is marked by the imposing summits of Scratchbury and Battlesbury Camps, the latter being the 'jewel' of hill-forts at 682 feet in height and virtually inaccessible on its north and north-east faces because of the steepness of the incline.

Warminster itself is a market town and also headquarters of the No. 1 School of Infantry, whose numerous barracks and workshops are served by rail sidings. Buses run from here to Longleat House, a big attraction for families wishing to see the beautiful gardens and wildlife park.

As the train leaves Warminster, the view to the west includes the strange conical Cley Hill, 784 feet in height, and in fine weather the Mendips in the distance, before the train descends Upton Scudamore Bank, through the tiny Dilton Marsh Halt, to arrive at the busy junction of Westbury. The route from here to Bristol is described in *South West by Rail*. You can also change trains for Swindon and Reading.

Fareham–Eastleigh
Returning to the earliest part of our route, let us join one of the hourly-running Portsmouth Harbour–Eastleigh diesel units at Fareham and pass on to the single-track section through Funtley Tunnel. In 1962, a landslip occurred on the up double-track avoiding line at Highlands Road, Fareham; with no money available to clear it the avoiding line was abandoned to assist the construction of the M27. The tunnel itself was upgraded and the line singled throughout from Fareham to Botley.

Emerging from the tunnel, we cross the River Meon, pass through another short tunnel at Tapnage and, in seven minutes and 5 miles after leaving Fareham, we run into Botley. This now-unstaffed station, was the junction for a 3¾-mile branch to Bishops Waltham which closed finally in 1962 except for a spur of about ⅓ mile used by the massive crushed-granite trains from Merehead Quarry, Somerset, serving a tarmac depot in what used to be Botley goods yard.

The village of Botley is ½ mile down the road and would be more pleasant if it were not for the heavy road traffic that passes through its centre. The famous writer, William Cobbett, lived here, and just across the road from the Botley flour-mills (which had a building mentioned in 'Domesday Book') is a small stone erected in his memory by the National Union of Journalists; my father, as Secretary to the Botley Labour Party, was instrumental in arranging for the memorial.

From Botley, our diesel pulls away through open country for the 5½-mile run to Eastleigh. About 2 miles west of Botley we pass the site of a new station, Hedge End North, to be completed in 1989, and serving the growing population being housed adjacent to the line. Hopefully third-rail electrification will have been authorised by then, giving passengers a through hourly service to Waterloo without changing; and one day, by changing at Eastleigh, onward services again to Chandlers Ford and Romsey.

SWINDON–WESTBURY
by Ian McGill

Our journey begins at Swindon, commercial and administrative heart of the modern borough of Thamesdown, and the largest town in Wiltshire. Melksham line trains usually leave from the bay platform (No. 3) at the 'country' end of the station and follow the mainline through Chippenham before heading south along some 9 miles of single track to join the Bath–Westbury line near Trowbridge.

The route between Chippenham and Westbury was one of the earliest railways in Wiltshire, opening as a broad-gauge line in 1848; but it has had a somewhat chequered history in recent years, losing two intermediate halts in 1955, while the remaining stopping services were withdrawn in April 1966. Thereafter only a few seasonal trains used the line as a convenient through route. Then even these spasmodic services ceased and the line was singled, carrying a diminishing number of freight-workings and diverted InterCity trains.

Closure seemed inevitable until, in 1985, increasing local pressure brought about the reopening of Melksham Station and reinstatement of a regular, if limited, passenger-train service under the provisions of the 1981 Amendment to the 1962 Transport Act. Unfortunately, the future of this experimental service is far from secure, and there is clearly a great deal of scope for a local rail-users' group to promote it, as is being effectively done in similar circumstances elsewhere.

At present, four trains a day in each direction serve Melksham; and could also serve Wootton Bassett, between Swindon and Chippenham, where there is also local pressure to reopen the station which closed in 1965. Parting company with the mainline to South Wales, which veers away to the right and round the western flank of the town, higher ground closes in on our route from the left, while opposite there are extensive views across an undulating pastoral landscape, punctuated at intervals by the farms and hamlets in the fertile upper reaches of the Bristol Avon and its tributaries.

Occasionally there are further glimpses of the old contour-hugging Wilts & Berks Canal, as it strives to maintain a course along the lower slopes of the high ground on the left until, sweeping round the hills below Lyneham, railway and canal are briefly united at Dauntsey Lock. Still clinging desperately to the hillside, the overgrown waterway meanders aimlessly away southwards, while our train hurries on across the valley, with the Church of Christian Malford prominent on the right, before encountering the Bristol Avon for the first time.

Soon after we cross the river, a curious elevated pathway will be seen on the left, beside a minor road at Kellaways. This is Maud Heath's Causeway, part of a paved footpath which dates from the fifteenth century, and which was provided through the generosity of a local market woman, to enable the country-folk to walk dry-shod to Chippenham Market.

We pass through a long cutting to emerge alongside the works of the Westinghouse Company, well-known manufacturers of railway brake and signalling equipment, at Chippenham. Once largely dependent on iron-founding and the cloth trade, Chippenham is a flourishing market town, whose centre is within a few minutes' walk of the station.

Chippenham is the nearest railhead for the picture-postcard village of Castle Combe and several equally attractive villages strung out along the southern slopes of the Cotswolds. But be warned — public transport facilities are minimal and intending visitors would do well to check bus services in advance, through the local Tourist Information Centre (telephone Chippenham 655864/657733).

Striding above the town on an impressive masonry viaduct, the railway continues on a lofty embankment for almost 2 miles, to reach Thingley Junction, where an isolated group of sidings alongside the up mainline serve a little-used railhead for Ministry of Defence establishments occupying many of the old Bath Stone workings which honeycomb the area. Curving away from the mainline and heading south along a single track, the train enters a cutting to emerge above the single street of Notton.

Passing the remains of Lacock Halt, the train descends towards Melksham via a series of cuttings and embankments. Intermittent views across the vale reveal the picturesque village of Lacock, some ¾ mile distant, nestling in the meadows of the valley floor, the slender spire of St Cyriac's Church piercing the distant green backdrop provided by Bewley Common, and the slopes of Bowden Hill beyond. Compact and largely medieval, Lacock is one of the gems among Wiltshire's many beautiful villages — mellow stone, dark timber framing, and warm brick providing a pleasing sense of homeliness and unity. Much of the thirteenth-century Lacock Abbey survives, carefully incorporated into a larger secular building by subsequent owners. William Henry Fox Talbot, acknowledged pioneer of modern photography, lived here and a museum devoted to his life and work has been created in the barn at the Abbey gates (to check opening times telephone 0747–840560).

Lacock has hourly buses on weekdays (Badgerline 234/237) serving Trowbridge, Melksham, and Chippenham. Melksham is the nearest station, and the most convenient for the bus, since the stops are only a short distance away in Beanacre Road. Hereabouts, the railway crosses, imperceptibly, the course of a Roman road and passes under a bridge where Beanacre Halt once stood. Beyond, Shaw Church dominates the distant scene and then, passing under Dunch Lane, the buildings of Melksham appear on either side.

The original station buildings have long since been demolished. The lights and bus-stop-type shelter have been provided with local financial assistance. To reach the town centre, walk along the short approach, and turn left, to negotiate a subway whose brightly painted murals include a tank locomotive and a High Speed Train, to emerge in Bath Road, which leads past the Avon Works complex to the town bridge and shops.

Although essentially an industrial town, perhaps best known as the home of Avon Rubber, Melksham nevertheless retains something of a traditional character through its older buildings, some of which are a legacy from the days when cloth-making was the key to local prosperity. An exploration on foot will reveal some handsome period buildings, and quiet picturesque corners like the City and Canon Square. Farther afield, the Spa Pump Room and a series of elegant houses intended for the accommodation of visitors are still to be found at the end of Spa Road, dating from the town's brief career as a spa in the early nineteenth century.

Quickly regaining open country, the B3107 runs alongside for a mile or so, between railway and river, finally crossing above the line to go its separate way near the site of Broughton Gifford Halt, which closed in 1955. Continuing across riverside meadows, we see the lonely little Church of Whaddon, standing in isolation at the end of a lane on the opposite bank of the Avon. A house standing adjacent to the line on the right was the residence of the station masters at Holt, and is the only substantial evidence of this station to survive.

Like many other local communities, Holt was once involved in the cloth trade and, although it is in a predominantly agricultural area, there is an industrial presence, including a long-established tannery and a bedding factory, which happen to be located in a street called 'The Midlands'. Unless and until its station is reopened, Holt can be reached by a Badgerline No. 237 bus which serves the village about every two hours.

Our journey continues across low-lying pasture-land and over the River Avon, passing Nestlé's factory on the right, and our train joins the Bath–Westbury route at the triangular Bradford Junction. The train passes beneath an aqueduct carrying the Kennet & Avon Canal and soon the buildings of Ushers Brewery and Bowyers meat products factory herald the approach to Trowbridge Station, whose Spartan, unkempt appearance is due to delayed rebuilding work.

Trowbridge can trace its origins back to Saxon times. It prospered as a major centre of the West of England cloth industry and the wealth generated by this trade has left some distinctive architectural work, from fine Georgian merchants' houses to humble weavers' cottages. Near the town bridge, with its adjacent lock-up, is a building which may well be unique. This is the Handle House, an unpretentious structure spanning the River Biss, whose walls were so constructed as to allow the free passage of air for the drying of teazels, which were used to raise the nap on cloth. It stands appropriately in the shadow of one of the surviving mill buildings.

A copy of the town guide, or town trail leaflet, will be of considerable value on a walk round the area. During the last century, Trowbridge was selected as the headquarters for Wiltshire County Council, despite rival claims, because of its favourable position on the railway network at that time. It has remained the administrative centre ever since. Isaac Pitman, inventor of a system of shorthand, was born here and the poet George Crabbe was Rector between 1814 and 1832. In the parish churchyard is the grave of young Thomas Helliker, a local cloth-worker who became a martyr to the cause of trade unionism. Arrested on the pretext of having threatened a watchman with a firearm, during anti-machinery riots in 1802, he refused to reveal the identity of the perpetrator, and was sentenced to death, being hanged on his nineteenth birthday.

Embarking on the final stage of our travel, the train wends its way past County Hall on the left; beyond the town, outlying development merges untidily with neighbouring villages, while ahead, the northern slopes of Salisbury Plain, swelling in whale-backed undulations from the clay vale below, draw steadily closer. The remaining miles are dominated by views of Westbury White Horse, cut into the chalk hillside on the left, before our train runs round the curve of a triangular junction to draw into the platform at Westbury Station.

The station is about a mile from Westbury town centre, at the end of a long curving approach road, and assumed its present form in 1900 when the original structure was rebuilt. Extensive sheets of water in the vicinity are a reminder that ironstone deposits were found near by when the railway was first constructed, and Westbury ironworks was established at a site just north of the station.

Apart from the Parish Church of All Saints, little of historic or architectural merit has survived in Westbury, although for much of its history the town was largely dependent upon the West of England cloth trade. Probably the most interesting of the remaining mill buildings is the main block of the Angel Mill complex which dates from 1807 and is considered to be the earliest textile factory in the district to have been purpose-built for steam-powered machinery.

For a description of the journeys onward to Weymouth and the West Country, see our companion volume, *South West by Rail.* You can also change at Westbury for the important cross-country route to Salisbury, Southampton, and Portsmouth, described on pages 31–35.

LONDON MARYLEBONE–BANBURY
by Derek Foster

Most of this line was built in the early 1900s as a joint line for the Great Western Railway and the Great Central Railway Companies. It gave the Great Western a shorter route from London to Birmingham and the Great Central an easier graded route from London to Sheffield and Manchester.

The straight flat track across the Vale of Aylesbury, in particular, enabled the GWR to compete effectively with the London & North Western Railway for traffic from

London to the West Midlands and beyond. Electrification of the rival ex-L&NWR route from Euston to Birmingham in the 1960s, however, led to a downgrading of this line, which served fewer large centres of population on the way.

The London Paddington–Birmingham trains which graced the line were gradually transferred to the Oxford route until in the 1970s all services bar one morning working and one evening return train were re-routed and replaced by DMUs running from London Marylebone to Banbury at approximately one every two hours. Even the Paddington–Birmingham working has now been cut back to start from Leamington Spa in the morning and terminate at Banbury in the evening. There has, however, been an increase recently in the numbers of trains from Marylebone to Aylesbury using this route as far as Princes Risborough, thus giving most stations along it an approximately hourly service, with extras at peak times.

The DMUs to Banbury share with Aylesbury via Amersham trains the same route out of Marylebone as far as Neasden South Junction before branching westwards past Wembley Stadium, where nearly all trains stop. The suburban landscape continues past Northolt Junction, where we join the Paddington line, and West Ruislip, which gives useful interchange with London Transport's Central Line.

Viaducts over the Grand Union Canal and River Colne bring us into Buckinghamshire and the start of open countryside. Denham, Gerrards Cross, and Beaconsfield have all become popular commuter areas in the wooded Chiltern Hundreds; while at the last-named, Beaconscot Model Railway and Village, just north of the station, is an added attraction for the visitor.

The 348-yard-long Whitehouse Farm Tunnel brings us into the Wycombe Valley. There are fine views across the valley before we draw into High Wycombe Station, set on the hillside overlooking this busy town of 60,000 people, well known for its furniture-making. The station is interesting in that the platforms are staggered, linked by a subway.

On leaving High Wycombe, the train passes a new supermarket, factories, and

The Marylebone–Banbury–Stratford-upon-Avon route is sometimes used by steam specials. Here, *Sir Nigel Gresley* heads a Pullman train through the Chilterns near Saunderton. (*Photo:* Nigel Hunt)

houses as the town slopes away to the left. The interesting building on the hill is West Wycombe House with its park, built in the 1700s by the Dashwood family and rebuilt in the 1750s: members of the family still reside here. It is open to the public, as are the nearby West Wycombe Caves. (For information, write to West Wycombe Park Office, West Wycombe, Bucks, HP14 3AJ; telephone 1049-24411/2.) Up on the wooded hillside is West Wycombe Church, recognisable by the ususual golden ball on its tower. West Wycombe Station was closed in 1958, and so visitors must now travel by bus or bicycle from High Wycombe.

The train heads up through the Chilterns and passes the little station of Saunderton, surrounded by factories but little else. Few trains call here, for the village is some distance away. Then the up line dips away into a cutting and passes through a tunnel. We are on a down gradient now, and the two lines do not link up again until the train reaches Princes Risborough. This station is a pale shadow of its former self, with only the up platform in use, and so our train has to cross to the up line.

As we leave Princes Risborough, branch lines run off to the left and right; those to the left going to Chinnor cement works and Thame oil terminal, while that to the right is the link to Aylesbury. The 7-mile single-track line to Aylesbury runs along the foot of the Chilterns, calling at two unstaffed halts before heading north across the Vale to rejoin the line from Marylebone via Amersham.

Our line to Banbury now becomes single track, the Chilterns are left behind and the train enters largely flat countryside. The chimneys of Chinnor cement works can be seen away to the left. A new housing development to the right signals the approach to the line's newest station, Haddenham and Thame Parkway, opened in October 1987. This smart station with a large car park serves the village of Haddenham and is on the bus route from Aylesbury to the market town of Thame, some 3 miles away across the border in Oxfordshire. Both Oxfordshire and Buckinghamshire County Councils helped to pay for this new station.

Some 3 miles farther along the line to the right can be seen an old embankment. This was part of Ashendon Junction, where the Great Central line to Grendon Underwood Junction went off under the embankment carrying the Great Western up line. Brill Hill is prominent to the left before the train passes through the 191-yard-long Brill Tunnel. Away to the right can be seen the chimneys of Calvert brickworks. The train crosses the A41 at Blackthorn and the Oxford-Bletchley line, now single track, and passes Bicester's industrial estate at Launton.

Our train arrives at Bicester North Station, which has two platforms, although only one is in use for much of the time. Bicester is a pleasant country town set to expand from its present population of 17,000 to 26,000 by 1996.

Leaving Bicester, the line passes over the Buckingham Road and then the A41 Banbury Road, with a rooftop view across the town. Some 2 miles farther on, the line enters a cutting. As we pass Ardley Quarry, notice the old rusted-up loading equipment. The train passes under two rows of landing lights for the RAF base at Upper Heyford, where F111 fighter bombers with their nuclear warheads are stationed.

The train then goes through another tunnel, under an extension of the Cotswold Hills, and as it emerges the Cherwell Valley unfolds to the left with the River Cherwell, the Oxford Canal, and the mainline from Oxford and the South. Our train passes over two viaducts. Barges on the canal can be seen and the old Aynho Station, now used as a coal yard. The line on which we are travelling passes over the Oxford line on a girder bridge before dropping down to join it.

The Oxford Canal and meandering River Cherwell keep company with the line as it approaches Kings Sutton Halt, serving a picturesque village dominated by a tall church spire just to the right. Most trains from Marylebone call here, arriving some six minutes later in Banbury Station, rebuilt in the late 1950s, largely of precast concrete, and now showing some signs of deterioration.

Banbury is the second largest town in Oxfordshire, with a population of approximately 38,000 and rapidly expanding. It was designated an overspill town in the 1960s and also saw an influx of Birmingham people when Alfred Bird & Sons (now General Foods) moved from the West Midlands.

The town has been immortalised in the nursery rhyme, 'Ride a cock-horse to Banbury Cross,/To see a fine lady upon a white horse.' Follow the signs to the Tourist Information Centre, in the Town Museum facing the Cross which was built in 1859 to celebrate the marriage of the Princess Royal to Frederick, Prince of Prussia. The statues of Queen Victoria, King Edward VII, and King George V were added in 1911.

There were three earlier crosses: White Cross in West Bar Street, Bread Cross in High Street, and the Market Cross, thought to have been in Cornhill, part of the Market Place. Here is the main entrance to the Castle shopping precinct, on the site of the old castle which was demolished in the Civil War by townsfolk to repair their own damaged properties. At the rear of the precinct is found the 'Modern Banbury Cross', a steel structure where a street market is held on Thursdays and Saturdays. (Early closing is on Tuesdays.)

Sample some Banbury cakes. Unfortunately, the original shop where these were baked was demolished a few years ago despite attempts to save it. Banbury also boasts the largest cattle market in Europe, has a good shopping centre and sports facilities including an indoor sports centre, outdoor swimming-pool, a football ground, a cricket pitch, bowls greens, and a Council-owned golf-course. Every October in the streets is the Michaelmas Fair, lasting three days.

Places of interest around Banbury include Broughton Castle – really a large manor house – and Sulgrave Manor, the ancestral home of George Washington. To the north-west is Edge Hill, where an outdoor museum is being established on the site of the famous battle in the Civil War. Unfortunately, country bus services in the area are poor – and so the best way to visit these places is to bring a bike!

LONDON MARYLEBONE–AYLESBURY
by Stephen Sykes

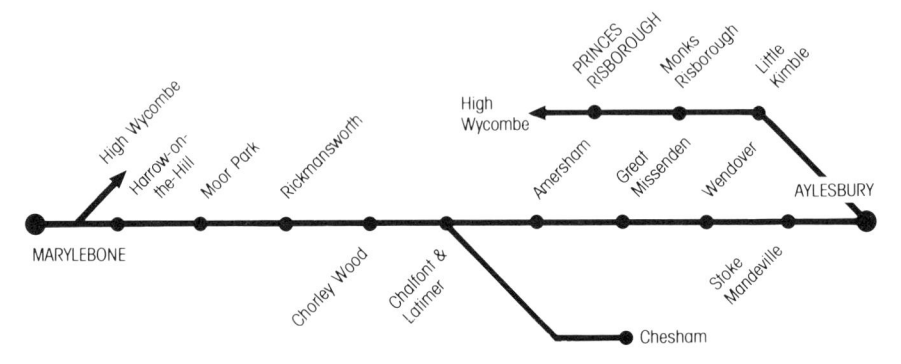

Train services between London, Amersham, and Aylesbury are operated by British Rail, with additional London Underground trains as far as Amersham. The BR service from Marylebone to Amersham and Aylesbury is basically hourly on weekdays, with trains calling at Harrow on the Hill and Moor Park, then all stations to Aylesbury. London Underground runs a half-hourly service on the Metropolitan Line from Baker Street and Finchley Road as far as Amersham, connecting at

Chalfont and Latimer with a shuttle service to Chesham. On Sundays, an hourly BR service runs between Aylesbury and Amersham, connecting there with Metropolitan Line trains to Baker Street.

British Rail trains depart from Marylebone Station, opened in 1899 as the London terminus of the Great Central Railway route from the Midlands. About 2 miles out of Marylebone, near Finchley Road Station, the BR line converges with the Metropolitan Line from Baker Street, and the lines then run together through the Metroland suburbs of north-west London, which developed after the arrival of the Metropolitan Railway in the 1880s and 1890s. Between Rickmansworth and Chorleywood, in an area of large houses in spacious, well-wooded gardens, the line passes under the M25 motorway. Immediately after leaving Chorleywood Station, the train enters Buckinghamshire and the Chiltern Hills.

The next station, Chalfont and Latimer, was originally a rural halt called Chalfont Road. The suburb which developed around the station became known as Little Chalfont, but the older villages of Chalfont St Giles and Chalfont St Peter are several miles away to the south. Chalfont and Latimer Station is the junction for the branch line to Chesham. The single-track branch runs alongside the mainline for about a mile, then curves away to the north and winds down through woodland to the valley of the River Chess, crossing the river just outside the town. Chesham has some historic buildings and a large public park near the town centre.

The mainline continues past further suburban housing to Amersham Station, the terminus for Metropolitan Line trains. To the north, beyond the station car park, can be seen the modern red-brick Civic Centre.

The area around the station, known as Amersham-on-the-Hill, developed after the railway arrived in 1892. Old Amersham, about a mile to the south of the station, in the Misbourne Valley, is well worth a visit. It can be reached by walking or taking a bus down Station Road, or by following a footpath which leads off Station Road to the west and down through Parsonage Wood to the church. Old Amersham is largely unspoilt by modern development and, now that there is a bypass, comparatively quiet. The main street has many seventeenth- and eighteenth-century buildings, including the red-brick and stone Market Hall. The parish church, near the river, contains some impressive monuments. There are gift and antique shops, and a museum run by the Amersham Society is open at summer week-ends.

Soon after leaving Amersham, the Aylesbury train begins the descent to the Misbourne Valley. For the first few miles, the line runs through woodland, but to the south there are occasional glimpses of the river and the main Uxbridge–Aylesbury road in the valley, and of the hills beyond. The large white building on the hillside above a lake is Shardeloes, an eighteenth-century mansion now converted into flats. As the train emerges from the woods, the village of Little Missenden can be seen in the valley. The line now crosses the main road and the river, and runs alongside them into Great Missenden. As the train approaches the station, the church is visible on the hillside to the east, and it is possible to glimpse the nineteenth-century buildings of Missenden Abbey, now used as a residential adult education centre.

Beyond Great Missenden, the line passes through rolling farmland, running close to the main road through the Wendover Gap. Just before the train reaches Wendover Station, the church can be seen through the trees to the east. Wendover has some interesting old buildings, a traditional tea-shop, and a street market on Thursdays. From the station approach road, the main street leads downhill to the Victorian clocktower, now used as a Tourist Information Centre and Parish Council offices.

The train emerges from the Chilterns and descends to the Vale of Aylesbury. To the south-west, on the summit of Coombe Hill, is an obelisk to the memory of local men killed in the Boer War. To the north-east, on the wooded slopes of Haddington Hill, are Halton House and the other buildings of Halton RAF Camp. The next station is

Stoke Mandeville. In the station forecourt, alongside the London-bound platform and visible from the train, is a garden containing a group of sculptures including the figure of one of the station staff, tending the garden, and two lions, one of whom has deserted his pedestal at the entrance to the garden and is investigating a flower-bed!

About a mile farther on, Stoke Mandeville Hospital is seen on the south-west side of the line. For the rest of the journey, the line is flanked by the housing estates, factories, and office blocks of Aylesbury. As the line curves round to enter the station, it is joined by a single-track line from the south. This is the former Great Western Railway line, which leaves the High Wycombe–Banbury line at Princes Risborough. The service on this line was improved in 1987, and there are now trains about every two hours on weekdays from Marylebone to Aylesbury via High Wycombe.

Aylesbury is the county town of Buckinghamshire, with a population of about 50,000. The view of the town centre from the railway station is not inviting: above a multi-storey car park can be seen the top few floors of the concrete tower block built in 1966 as County Council offices. However, beyond the inner ring road, and the concrete of the 1960s redevelopment area, some attractive parts of the town remain. In the old Market Square, a number of interesting buildings have been spared, including the eighteenth-century County Hall. The area around the parish church and the Buckinghamshire County Museum is a quiet backwater, hardly touched by modern development. There is a Tourist Information Centre in the new County offices.

Until 1966, passenger trains continued beyond Aylesbury to Brackley, Rugby, Leicester, and Nottingham, on the former Great Central Railway route. A small part of this route survives as a goods line through Quainton Road and Calvert, joining the Bicester–Bletchley line at Claydon Junction, about 12 miles from Aylesbury. The former station at Quainton Road is now the Buckinghamshire Steam Centre, housing a large collection of locomotives and rolling-stock. On Bank Holiday Mondays between Easter and August, special trains run from Aylesbury to the Steam Centre.

Quainton Road Steam Centre. (*Photo:* Thames & Chilterns Tourist Board)

OXFORD–BICESTER TOWN
by Nicholas Medley

The railway line between Oxford and Bicester is once again featured on British Rail maps, having been reopened to passengers on an experimental basis in May 1987, after a gap of nearly twenty years.

Originally opened in 1847 as part of the London & North West Railway's through route between the university cities of Oxford and Cambridge, the section in question was closed with effect from 1 January 1968.

Today it is very much a basic railway. Reduced to single track in 1973, it has minimal signalling, severe speed restrictions, and no run-round facilities at Bicester. Consequently, the 11¾-mile journey presently takes about twenty-five minutes.

On leaving Oxford Station, the former Great Western Railway mainline is followed for about 1½ miles to the present-day connection with the L&NWR route. At the north end of the station the line passes over the channel linking the River Thames with the Oxford Canal, and the remains of the line from the L&NWR Rewley Road terminus, closed to passengers in 1951, can be observed on the right. As it was on a slightly lower level than the GWR at this point, it crossed the channel by means of a swing bridge which, although now out of use, is to be preserved.

Beyond the junction with the mainline, we cross the Oxford Canal. This is the residential part of North Oxford, and the playing-fields of St Edward's School can be seen on the right. Soon the line enters a cutting leading to the only tunnel, albeit a very modest affair 140 yards in length, which takes the line under the main A40 road forming the northern section of Oxford's ring road.

Shortly after leaving the tunnel, the line is bordered by the large Pear Tree park-and-ride. This has been suggested as the site for a new station.

The route soon assumes a more rural character. The remainder of the journey to Bicester is across flat, open country, the River Cherwell being crossed shortly before Islip. Birthplace of Edward the Confessor, Islip is a picturesque village, situated away from the main road. The former station here was of largely timber construction, and alas, all traces of it have now been erased. Once the present service becomes established, however, it is hoped that a new halt will be built here.

The line now skirts the northern fringe of Otmoor, a curiously isolated area of some 4,000 acres uncrossed by any roads. It has, however, recently been threatened by the Birmingham extension of the M40 motorway. The small villages of Oddington, Charlton-on-Otmoor, Fencott, and Murcott are reminiscent of East Anglia and well worth a visit. As might be expected, this is ideal cycling country!

The last 4 miles or so into Bicester are virtually dead straight. Half a mile before the station, the entrance to the Bicester Military Railway can be seen on the south side of the line. This extensive system, built in the early days of the Second World War to serve the large ordnance depot, encircles two low-lying hills in the area and has some 40 miles of track.

Bicester Town Station – formerly known as 'London Road' – now freshly painted in the colours of Network South East, is currently the end of the line for passengers. However, for those wishing to travel on by train, Bicester North Station on the Marylebone–Banbury route is about ¾ mile distant, on the other side of the town centre. Bicester itself has a three-cornered area with an interesting building which was formerly the Town Hall. Also worthy of visit is the Parish Church of St Edburg, which possesses some fine monuments and medieval carvings and is approached along a street with some handsome old stone houses.

On to Milton Keynes?
The cross-country rail routes from Oxford and Aylesbury via Winslow to Milton

Keynes must surely have one of the best cases for reopening to through passenger traffic of any in South East England.

When the Oxford–Bletchley line closed to passengers at the end of 1967, Milton Keynes as a city did not exist. The main town in the area, Bletchley, had a population of about 20,000. Today the new city and its environs has approximately 150,000 inhabitants, while Oxford has approaching 100,000 and Aylesbury 50,000. Despite this, public transport between these large centres and the villages around varies from poor to non-existent.

A glance at any rail map reveals a complete lack of any east–west connections in this part of the country. The prospective rail traveller from Oxford to Milton Keynes, for instance, has the choice of going via Coventry or through London, both options equally unattractive in terms of both time and cost. The only other alternative is to use the infrequent and lengthy bus service.

Reopening this line would, therefore, serve a triple purpose. Firstly, it would greatly facilitate communications between Milton Keynes with its large modern shopping complex, Aylesbury – the county town and administrative centre of Buckinghamshire, and Oxford with its huge tourist market, major regional hospitals, and new ice-rink. Secondly, it would provide much-needed local transport in this still largely rural area of North Buckinghamshire. Finally, it would provide an important cross-country link, allowing journeys between such places as Northampton and Bristol without the need to travel via London with its attendant change of stations.

For these reasons, the RDS called a series of meetings which resulted in the formation, in March 1987, of the Oxon and Bucks Rail Action Committee, co-ordinating the efforts of several interested bodies to secure the restoration of this link to the rail network.

OXFORD–WORCESTER (THE COTSWOLD LINE)

by Oliver Lovell

The Oxford–Worcester Railway – known as 'the Cotswold line' – has a rich, varied, and interesting history. The first attempt at a rail link between the growing industrial Midlands and the Thames at Oxford was the construction, in 1826, of a horse-drawn tramway running southwards from the Stratford-upon-Avon terminus of the canal from Birmingham towards Oxford. As with many schemes of the era, it failed to achieve its ambition and only reached as far as Moreton-in-Marsh.

The Oxford, Worcester & Wolverhampton Railway – nicknamed the 'Old Worse & Worse' – opened nearly thirty years later, purportedly as a mixed-gauge line, this time fulfilling the role the tramway failed to achieve. The route was to become part of the Great Western Railway empire and, with railway mania rampant, the extensive stage-coach runs were totally wiped out within three years. The expanding railway company planned to build workshops and repair depots half-way along the line at Moreton, but so vociferous was the local opposition that the scheme was dropped and the works finally sited at Swindon.

Now shorn of its branches and cross routes, the Cotswold line remains to fulfil the vital role of linking London and the Thames Valley with the West Midlands, Malverns, and Hereford. Most trains run between Hereford, Worcester, and Oxford, though there are a number of direct InterCity 125 trains to and from Paddington. Certain local services call at the Oxfordshire halts. For fuller details of the line's history refer to *Oxford–Hereford Line*, No. 5 in the series *Western at Work* by Geoffrey Body, MCIT, published jointly by BR Western and Avon-Anglia Publications.

Our Worcester-bound train leaves the Birmingham route at Wolvercote Junction, 3 miles north of Oxford, and branches westwards on to the largely single-track 55-mile-long Cotswold line – a route full of scenic and historic interest.

Of the seven stations in Oxfordshire, only Charlbury and Kingham remain staffed. The rest were reduced to basic halts in the 1960s, having only just escaped closure under Dr Beeching's 'Axe'. A mile or so beyond Wolvercote is Yarnton which, along with the Fairford branch, still clearly visible, was closed in 1962.

The first halt reached is Handborough which, in 1965, received the funeral train carrying the body of Sir Winston Churchill who lies buried in Bladon churchyard, barely a mile from the station. In the early days of the line, Handborough served through trains running to Euston via a direct spur on to the Bicester line. In those days the station even boasted a refreshment room. At the far end of the yard is a bus museum (for details telephone Enstone 8739).

From here, a walk of 2 miles brings one to Blenheim Palace and its park and gardens. This magnificent estate – the seat of the Dukes of Marlborough and named to commemorate the victory, in 1704, at Blenheim in Bavaria – is most certainly worth a visit. Details of dates and hours of opening can be obtained from the Chief Guide's Office at Blenheim Palace (telephone 0993–811325).

The train now runs through the gentle and most attractive valley of the River Evenlode – a twisting and turning tributary of the Thames. In all, it is crossed and recrossed by the railway no fewer than eleven times before Charlbury is reached.

A mile beyond Handborough is the little halt of Combe, built (along with Finstock)

The grounds of Blenheim Palace. (*Photo:* Thames & Chilterns Tourist Board)

in the 1930s to counter growing road competition. Neither station was ever staffed. Across the line by Combe Station lies an attractive stone-built saw-mill – the site of a mill is listed in 'Domesday Book' in 1086. Its water-wheel was supplemented by an 1852 beam-engine now restored and 'in steam' on certain Sundays (for details telephone 08675–2652).

Bridges over the Evenlode now follow in quick succession and some 2 miles beyond Combe the North Leigh Roman Villa site may be glimpsed in a field to the west of the line. Deer from Cornbury Park Estate graze near by.

Next comes Finstock, with its new platform constructed shortly after the single track was slewed from the old up platform in the mid 1980s. As with Combe, the Cotswold Line Promotion Group celebrated the fiftieth birthday of this station in grand style with hot punch, bunting, hanging baskets, a band, and Morris dancers.

Just beyond Finstock lies Cornbury Park – the home of Lord Rotherwick – and the secretive Wychwood Forest, once very extensive and a favourite hunting-ground of Henry VIII. At the time of writing, the forest is only accessible to the public on Palm Sunday each year. The train enters a cutting through the park grounds and emerges to cross the Evenlode once again, then slows to stop at Charlbury Station.

The original Brunellian Swiss chalet-type station building has been sympathetically renovated and is fondly cared for by station staff and the local community alike. Great Western Railway seats and station nameboards, neat flower-beds, and a stone-bordered goldfish-pond complete the picture which, at a quiet time, takes one's mind back to the hiss of steam and a country railway of bygone days.

Charlbury Station is, however, by no means a sleepy one, as the large – and invariably full – car park on the site of the former goods sidings will testify. Morning and evening, the platform is crowded with daily commuters who work in Oxford, Reading, or London. At such times of bustling activity, it is ironic to reflect that this station once featured on Dr Beeching's long list of proposed closures. The village, just up the hill, is quiet and most attractive, and from it one can ideally explore the area on foot or by cycle.

The line – still on the climb – now enters flatter and less-wooded countryside and after a further 4 miles reaches Ascott-under-Wychwood. Here there is a modest halt and a signal-box controls entry to an 11-mile double section of track ending at Moreton-in-Marsh. Next comes Shipton, formerly Shipton for Burford which, now shorn of its station building, signal-box, goods shed, and once-busy sidings, possesses only a small bus-stop-type shelter.

One and a half miles north of Shipton, the train crosses Bruern Road. Recent modernisation rendered the signal-box redundant and it has now been replanted in the garden of a nearby lineside house. The road crossing is now monitored by closed-circuit television controlled from Ascott box. Through the trees, Bruern Abbey may just be glimpsed as the train crosses this minor road.

A further mile brings the line to Kingham, where all trains stop. Until closure in the 1960s of the Cheltenham and Chipping Norton lines, Kingham was a busy interchange station which, before 1906, was known as 'Chipping Norton Junction'. The former station buildings were hastily demolished in the mid 1970s to thwart – it was said – the placing on them of a preservation order. The new construction is quite adequate but lacks character. The railway footbridge once extended right into the gardens of the former imposing Langston Arms Hotel. Once a hunting-lodge, it recently became a home for the elderly.

The village of Kingham lies about a mile to the east. The churchyard at Idbury, a pretty hill village almost within sight of Kingham, contains the grave of Sir Benjamin Baker, one of the two Chief Engineers of the Forth Railway Bridge; the other being Sir John Fowler who was closely involved in the construction of the Cotswold line. It is appropriate that his colleague should lie in such close proximity.

The Oxfordshire/Gloucestershire county boundary is reached at Adelstrop and the station itself – immortalised by Edward Thomas in his evocative poem: 'Yes, I remember Adelstrop' – might still have been open for business today had it been situated south of the main road bridge in Oxfordshire. All the Beeching-threatened stations on the line in this county were reprieved largely through the actions of an Oxfordshire-based rail-user group. Not far from the station site, the old GWR seat and nameboard which once graced the station has been preserved in the village bus shelter. The seat now bears a plaque on which Edward Thomas's poem appears in full.

Continuing its gentle climb, the line passes close to Daylesford Church. Built by Warren Hastings – once Governor-General of India – it bears a distinctly Oriental look. Westward, Stow-on-the-Wold can be clearly seen, its church prominent on the 'wold' or hill some 4 miles away. Stow has a truly mellow Cotswold flavour and is noted for its horse fairs and many antique shops. It can easily be reached by bus from Moreton-in-Marsh, the next station on the line. Pulham & Sons (telephone Bourton-on-the-Water 20369) run buses several times a day, continuing to picturesque Bourton and down to Cheltenham.

Moreton, once the junction with the Shipston on Stour branch (closed to passengers as long ago as 1929 and to freight in 1960), is a purposeful little station which serves a bustling, growing town on the Fosse Way with a large Tuesday market. Moreton Station is a useful stop-off point for exploring the Cotswolds by bus, bicycle, or on foot. There is a cycle hire facility in the High Street (Toy & Cycle Shop, telephone 0608–50756). Tourist information is available in the Council offices and Library.

The line reaches its summit in Dorn Cutting and, passing a mile to the east of the fine old wool town of Chipping Campden, the train enters the first tunnel on the line. Beyond, down Campden Bank, is laid before it the county of Worcestershire and the extensive Vale of Evesham. This flat and intensive fruit- and vegetable-growing area contrasts strongly with the gently undulating Cotswolds. Here, the building material is brick – again in striking contrast with the mellow stone previously encountered.

Four miles beyond the tunnel is Honeybourne, once a large and important junction station which closed with its last connecting line, to Stratford, in 1969 but happily was resurrected in 1981 with the active support of the Cotswold Line Promotion Group.

The train is shortly to cross the Shakespeare Avon and stop at Evesham which, lying in a loop of the river, is the largest intermediate town on the line. Six miles beyond, and still in the fertile vale, is Pershore Station with its service much enhanced in recent years. The station is some way from the town and its famous abbey, but a minibus service links with most daytime trains.

The Bredon Hills can now be seen to the south and the impressive Malverns loom ahead across the River Severn. The train leaves the Cotswold line at Norton Junction and heads north to Worcester Shrub Hill Station – the junction for Cheltenham, the South West, and some trains to Birmingham. Most trains from Oxford continue to Great Malvern and Hereford and those wishing to visit the many attractions that Worcester has to offer are advised to alight at Foregate Street Station which is conveniently situated in the very heart of the city. Worcester and the other lines serving it are described in our companion volume, *Midlands by Rail*.

TWYFORD–HENLEY ON THAMES
by Sue Cooper

Henley on Thames is reached by a 4½-mile branch from the mainline at Twyford. The line was built in 1857 and was once double track, with some through trains from London, but was singled in 1961. Nowadays it is served by a DMU shuttle, at least once per hour, connecting with a further DMU at Twyford and bringing Henley to just over an hour's journey time from London. The town has become popular with city commuters as well as being a favourite tourist destination, and the train is an ideal way of travelling there.

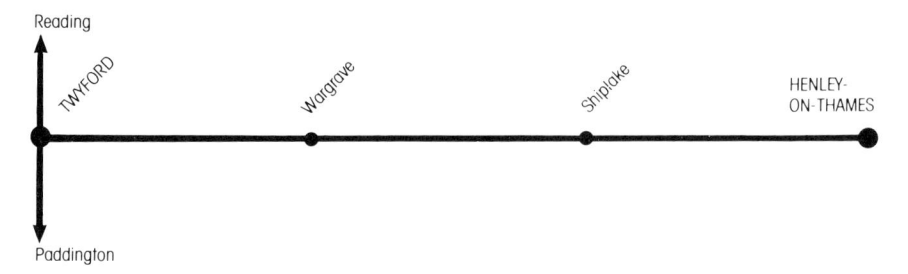

The first station on the branch is Wargrave, serving a pretty riverside village with some half-timbered houses. A bridge then carries the line over the Thames and ¼ mile farther on we stop at Shiplake Station, in the middle of a large village whose desirable residences nestle among trees on the left bank of the river. The former goods yard is now a station car park and the shelter on the platform is modern.

The train continues over an open crossing with flashing lights and runs close to the river for the remaining 1¾ miles to the terminus, whose modern brick building blends quite nicely with the older-style platform canopy. To the right are delightful riverside gardens, while a few minutes' walk brings you into the centre of the town.

In years gone by, Henley was a staging-post on the main road to Oxford and there are several inns from the coaching era where you can enjoy a drink and a meal in genuine old-world surroundings. A handsome five-arch stone bridge spans the Thames, dating from 1786 when Henley had become a fashionable resort. The parish church goes back to the thirteenth century and its distinctive tower dominates the town centre. You may not expect to find a theatre in a town of 11,000 people – but Henley has one, the Kenyon Theatre in New Street, not far from the local brewery.

Henley on Thames is most famous for its Royal Regatta, dating back to 1839 and bringing thousands of rowing enthusiasts and high society people here in the first week of July every year. When the water is less crowded, why not continue your exploring by taking a steamer trip down river, round the great bend to Marlow, and return by train on that other scenic branch that runs into this beautiful stretch of the Thames Valley?

MAIDENHEAD–MARLOW
by Nigel Hunt

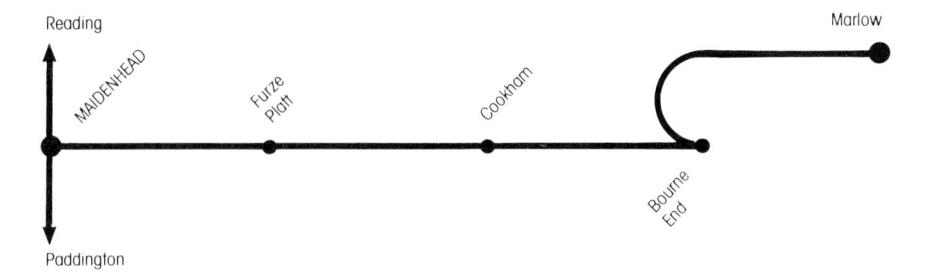

There are now few routes in Britain which provide the air of a typical branch line but travelling the 7¼ miles from Maidenhead to Marlow can still give that impression: a short journey of only twenty-four minutes through mainly rural scenery.

During 1854 the Wycombe Railway Company opened a 10-mile-long broad-gauge line from Maidenhead to High Wycombe, with stations at Boyn Hill (Maidenhead), Cookham, Marlow Road (now Bourne End), Wooburn Green, and Loudwater. With the exception of Boyn Hill, buildings were of attractive Chiltern brick and flint style.

Subsequent developments included closure of Boyn Hill, associated with the relocation of Maidenhead Station to the existing site in 1871, a rebuilding of the track to standard gauge in 1870, and the erection of Furze Platt Halt in 1937 to serve residential expansion in North Maidenhead.

The 2¾-mile-long branch from Bourne End to Marlow was opened in 1873 and trains along it are known locally as 'Marlow Donkeys' – an allusion to the old steam-engines which used to shuffle along the line, and believed to be synonymous with the small beasts which once hauled barges along this stretch of the Thames.

Steam locomotives continued to appear on the branches until 1966, though DMUs had first appeared on passenger trains in 1959. Unfortunately, cutting of costs was not sufficient to save through workings to High Wycombe, which ceased in 1970. The former trackbed north of Bourne End has been utilised for property developments at various points, but small sections at Bourne End and Loudwater may still be used as footpaths, providing access to more traditional footpaths from the Flackwell Heath and Wooburn areas. Access from Bourne End to High Wycombe is still possible by the Bee Line service No. 317 bus which operates at frequent intervals.

Leaving Maidenhead, our train climbs through a wooded cutting, past a variety of residential developments to Furze Platt. Open country follows with views across the fields to Taplow, and to Cliveden House set among the woods of the Chilterns. Cookham Station is next, and serves a pleasant riverside village. After passing

Marlow–Maidenhead train near Bourne End. (*Photo:* Nigel Hunt)

through Winter Hill Cutting the line emerges on an embankment which, as it drops down towards Bourne End, provides excellent views of Cockmarsh and Winter Hill (owned by the National Trust) before crossing the River Thames on a large iron bridge.

Immediately beyond is Bourne End Station, once a junction but now a terminus with two platforms. Our train reverses out of the station round a tight curve for the final leg of the journey to Marlow, at river-level, with the Thames on one side — with wooded hills beyond — and gravel pits on the other. Marlow's present station is a single platform and shelter; but just beyond it the memory of the 'Marlow Donkey' is perpetuated in the nearby public house.

A short walk along Station Road brings us to the centre of Marlow, where the broad High Street leads down to the handsome parish church beside the Thames and a fine suspension bridge built in 1831. The town contains many interesting old buildings dating from the seventeenth century onwards and leaflets to guide you round it can be obtained from the Tourist Information caravan in the riverside Higginson Park or from the Tourist Information Centre at the Council Offices, High Wycombe.

Trains, mostly two coaches, run an hourly service, including summer Sundays, with some peak-hour variations during the week. Stations at Cookham and Furze Platt are staffed on weekday mornings only, while Bourne End is staffed each morning except Sunday. Guards issue tickets on the train at other times. All signal-boxes have been demolished, the line being controlled by a token system from Slough panel box. Level crossings are of the modern, ungated, light-controlled variety. Bourne End ground frame, operated by the train's guard, controls movements to Marlow.

Both the Chiltern Society and Ramblers' Association have ensured that walkers and ramblers are catered for, with several well-defined footpaths in the area (consult Ordnance Survey maps: Landranger 175 or Pathfinder SU88/98). Widbrook, Cockmarsh, Winter Hill, Little Marlow, and Sheepbridge present excellent walks. Numerous hostelries, within easy reach of stations and footpaths, provide a variety of food and drink. There are towpath walks beside the Thames, but foot-bridges have to be erected at Temple and Bourne End to complete the Thames Path through the area. Boulter's, Marlow, and Temple Locks are popular places to watch river-boat activity. Cyclists will find stations convenient starting-points; our trains still carry bicycles. For photographers and artists the area has much to offer; landscape, architecture, and water at their British best, with the Stanley Spencer Gallery at Cookham well worth visiting.

For people who enjoy travelling on water, cruisers may be hired at Bourne End and rowing-boats are available at Cookham and Marlow. An ideal leisurely way to see the area is to take a trip on one of Salter's steamers, which run in summer from Marlow to Henley or Maidenhead and Windsor. There is a bus service from High Wycombe to Reading via Marlow and Henley; and a summer open-top bus from Windsor to Marlow via Maidenhead (for details telephone Maidenhead 21344).

WINDSOR
by John Bye

Windsor is the most popular tourist centre in Southern England outside London. It has two thriving railway stations, both termini, named Windsor and Eton Central (Western Region) and Windsor and Eton Riverside (Southern Region).

The ex-Great Western Railway station called Central is at the end of a 2¾-mile branch from the railhead at Slough on the Western Region mainline. There are no intermediate stations on the branch, which was opened on 10 October 1849 to Brunel's broad gauge. Standard gauge was added in 1862, after which the 'third rail' was removed on 30 June 1883. The engineer's original station was replaced by the current building in 1897, its four platforms were reduced to one in the 1968 resignalling scheme, but the refreshment room and booking-office still operate.

Madame Tussaud's took over Platforms 2–4 in 1983 to celebrate Queen Victoria's 1897 Diamond Jubilee of accession to the throne of the United Kingdom. The exhibition also houses some original railway coaches and a locomotive replica as well as original signposting, adverts, and timetables!

The current train service is operated by two- or three-car DMU at half-hourly intervals with rush-hour extras. Good connections are made at Slough for stations to Paddington, Reading, Didcot, Oxford, South Wales, and Avon.

The largest engineering structure is the approximately 1¾-mile viaduct (brick arched from 1865) at the Windsor end. This also includes the 202-foot three-bow-and-string girder bridge over the River Thames. Good views can be had of Windsor Castle and Eton College to the east.

The ex-London & South Western Railway station is Riverside, at the end of a branch from Staines, 6¼ miles distant. It opened on 1 December 1849 and for most of its life has been operated by through trains from London Waterloo. The present 1851 station survives almost unscathed with its three platforms but no refreshment rooms. The old Royal waiting-rooms, adjacent to the station in Datchet Road are now privately owned and the tower was used as a lookout for approaching Royal customers.

The present train service is operated by Class 455 electric multiple units. Third-rail electrification replaced steam on 6 July 1930 (eleven days before the author's birth). Like the Western Region branch, this one also enjoys a half-hour daily service travelling via Richmond and one train per hour via the Hounslow loop on Sundays.

The major engineering structure *en route* is Black Potts Bridge over the River Thames, dating from 1892. Of the three intermediate stations, Wraysbury,

Royalty and Railways Exhibition in the Royal Waiting-Room, Windsor and Eton Central. (Photo: Thames & Chilterns Tourist Board)

Sunnymeads, and Datchet, Sunnymeads was added later in the period. All are unstaffed at present. Windsor Castle is viewed to the west on this line; and to the south, across Home Park, on approach to Riverside Station.

On both routes, gradients are almost level. Day return tickets, Day Capital Cards, singles and seasons are interchangeable. There are good bus and coach services from Windsor in all directions and a regular double-deck open-topped circular local trip with commentary.

Apart from the castle and its ornate St George's Chapel, attractions for the visitor include the Market Cross House, the Guildhall (with its four pillars just short of the roof!), Marina, Racecourse, Safari Park, Great Park, Long Walk, and Art Centre. Boat trips are available on the River Thames (don't forget the ducks and swans!). Windsor Bridge – built in 1823 – has been pedestrianised since 1965 and brings you into Eton High Street with its antique shops, and to the famous College upon whose playing-fields, we are told, the Battle of Waterloo was won.

ASCOT/GUILDFORD–READING
by Peter Scott

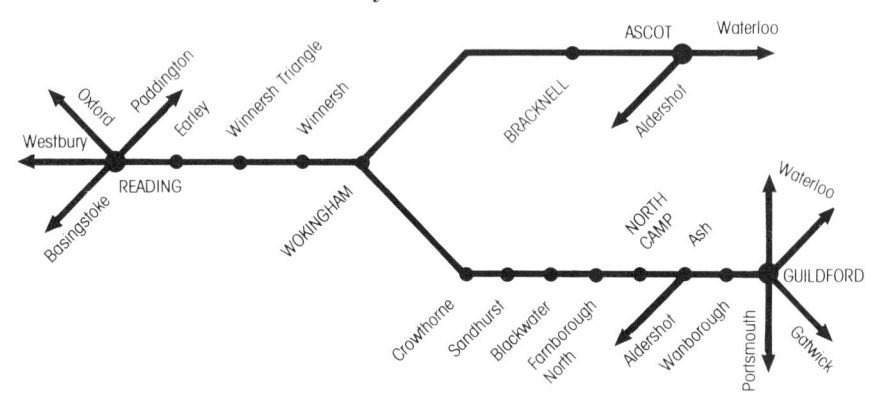

It was the South Eastern Railway that broke the Great Western Railway's monopoly at Reading, when they opened their line from Guildford and Redhill in July 1849. Passenger traffic on the line must have been fairly sparse, for at that time Wokingham was the only settlement of any size the railway passed between Reading and Guildford.

Wokingham became a junction in July 1856 when the London & South Western Railway opened their line from there through Ascot to Staines, to join the line to Waterloo.

The forward-looking Southern Railway, which took over from the South Eastern and London & South Western Railways in 1923, electrified the Reading–Waterloo line in 1939, using their standard third-rail system. The Wokingham–Guildford line remained steam operated until 1965 when British Railways introduced diesel units.

The basic pattern of services remained constant for many years: half-hourly Reading–Waterloo and hourly Reading–Guildford, and indeed still stands today, except that an hourly Reading–Gatwick service via Guildford is also operated. During the morning peaks extra trains operate to and from Waterloo, but in recent years the commuter flow into Reading on both lines has boomed, and the service has improved to show this. The stations between Wokingham and Reading now see a fifteen-minute-interval service into Reading in the morning peak.

The railway, by providing a quick and easy way into and out of Reading and London has capitalised on the tremendous amount of new housing in the Earley and Winnersh areas (one of the biggest developments in Europe) and an adjacent new industrial estate by opening a new station called Winnersh Triangle. Another new station is planned between Bracknell and Ascot at Martins Heron to serve new housing there. Emmbrook, between Winnersh and Wokingham, is also a possible site for a new station.

Leaving Waterloo, the 'Windsor lines' as they are known, which lead eventually to Reading, are lost in a maze of track. This maze becomes more complicated at Clapham Junction, the world's busiest junction with excellent connections for Gatwick Airport, Hastings, Eastbourne, Littlehampton, Brighton, and Portsmouth, to name but a few.

Richmond also offers good connections, including the London Transport District Line and the North London Line to North Woolwich. Twickenham is only served by Reading trains during rugby matches, for which extra coaches are normally added. Staines is the junction for Windsor, but also provides an interchange for people travelling to and from suburban stations not served by Reading trains.

The line continues now through Virginia Water, where Windsor Great Park and Virginia Water itself are about a mile away, and Sunningdale to reach Ascot. Here a line diverges, served by Ascot–Guildford trains via Camberley and Aldershot. Race specials are still run during Ascot Week.

Departing we pass through some pleasant woodland before seeing the extensive new housing development at Martins Heron, for which a new station has been proposed.

Bracknell, a New Town, has grown enormously and the station is one of the busiest on the line. We now run through some open countryside to pass Wokingham football ground and join the line from Guildford to arrive at Wokingham. This station remains as important as ever and provides a railhead for nearby Barkham and for several schools.

Winnersh has had its platforms recently extended to eight coach lengths, and similar work has been carried out at Wokingham and Bracknell. Winnersh Triangle opened in May 1986, and as well as serving the industrial complex also serves as a park-and-ride for Lower Earley and parts of Woodley.

Earley Station retains its original South Eastern station building and is worth a second glance. It has been recently refurbished. There is space for a hundred cycles here now and the racks are full every morning.

The line as it approaches Reading passes the remains of Huntley & Palmers biscuit factory. The Southern Railway station closed in 1965, but its site is now being used for the new development, long overdue for such a busy station.

Most local services towards Reading now start from Guildford, as regrettably, the intermediate stations towards Redhill only see odd trains outside the peak hours. Nevertheless, the Gatwick trains run through, and the line between Guildford and Redhill provides some glorious views of the North Downs as it passes through Reigate, Betchworth, Dorking, Gomshall, and Chilworth. Many interesting walks can be made from this stretch of the line, including the North Downs Way. Connections are available at Guildford to Portsmouth, the South Coast, and the Isle of Wight. Leaving Guildford the Reading line turns to leave the mainline towards Woking and Waterloo, and curves west past the University of Surrey and the cathedral.

Passing through Wanborough the line runs parallel to and at the foot of the Hogs Back, part of the North Downs. Just beyond Ash Station the line to Aldershot carries a Guildford to Ascot service via Aldershot and Camberley. This line is electrified, but our route onwards to Wokingham is diesel only. North Camp, the only station between Guildford and Wokingham to be served by the Gatwick trains, is much used by service personnel. There is also an oil depot here.

The line now crosses under the main Waterloo–Bournemouth line to reach Farnborough North. The famous air show brings many extra customers here.

Beyond Blackwater, at Sandhurst, we leave the Blackwater Valley, which we have been following since Ash. Crowthorne Station is located near the National Trust's Finchampstead Ridges and Wellington College. The line now runs through woodlands to reach the junction with the Ascot line at Wokingham.

MID HANTS RAILWAY
(THE WATERCRESS LINE)

Every hour throughout the day you can catch an electric train from London Waterloo, which will take you via Woking and Aldershot to Alton, a commuter town in northeast Hampshire. At Alton Station you can alight from your modern electric and, at Platform 3, join a vintage steam train for a 9½-mile journey through pleasant countryside to Alresford. The line crosses the Hampshire Downs, often through steep chalk cuttings and you can see many varieties of wild flowers by the lineside. As the line descends towards Alresford, there can be seen some of the watercress-beds which have given the line its name.

The line used to continue to Winchester, before its closure in the early 1970s; and has been reopened in stages by voluntary labour over the last ten years. It has some ten steam locomotives and a few diesels, some of which can be seen under restoration at the intermediate station of Ropley. Alresford Station is the headquarters of the preservation society and its associated company, and contains a shop and a museum.

There is a bus link between Alresford and Winchester, operated by the Alder Valley Company. Buses run hourly on weekdays and two-hourly on Sundays. (For details of the buses telephone Aldershot 23322; and for details of the steam trains telephone Alresford (0962-73) 3810.)

Steam and diesel trains meet at Medstead and Four Marks Station on the Mid Hants Railway. (*Photo: Tom Heavyside*)

ISLE OF WIGHT
by Paul Scott and Martin Heys

RYDE PIERHEAD — RYDE ESPLANADE — St. Johns Road — Brading — SANDOWN — Lake — SHANKLIN

Welcome to the Isle of Wight and its chief railway – Ryde Rail. Ryde pier head is the disembarkation point for Sealink ferries from Portsmouth Harbour. The pier was a major factor in the growth of Ryde in the last century. After the purchase of Osborne House by Queen Victoria, the Island soon became a fashionable watering-place of the Victorians.

The first thing you will notice about the trains is a certain similarity to those operated by the London Underground, and nothing like any other BR trains which may have brought you to Portsmouth Harbour. These are in fact ex-London Transport Tube trains, dating back to 1924, the most modern coach having been built in 1934. They were transferred to the Island after the cessation of steam trains in 1966/67.

Soon after leaving Ryde pier head on your right you will see the remains of the Ryde Pier Tramway. Before the railway was completed between Ryde St John's Road and Ryde Esplanade, the tramway connected these two stations.

We are now approaching Ryde Esplanade, which has always been considered the gateway to the Island. The Southern Vectis bus terminal is just outside, and on the other side of the railway line is the Hovercraft with frequent services to Southsea.

Walk along the sea-front towards Ryde Pavilion and bowling-green with its children's playground and you will eventually come to the canoe-lake. Just over the road is the fine sandy beach of Appley. A walk in the other direction up and along Union Street will bring you to the fine shopping area of the town. While in Union Street, look out for the finely restored Royal Victoria Arcade.

Back at Ryde Esplanade, you can book a coach tour excursion, or perhaps a trip on the Solent on a Blue Funnel cruiser. The Tourist Information Office here offers advice on all activities taking place on the Island. If the weather is not so good, catch a bus to Westridge Leisure Centre with its excellent sports facilities, including a large indoor swimming-pool and the Cothey Bottom Heritage Centre.

Back now to our train journey to Shanklin. As we leave Ryde Esplanade, the train descends towards the tunnel, built so that the railway could not be seen from the town. Going round some tortuous bends, it eventually leads us to Ryde St John's Road Station, where the maintenance is carried out on all Ryde Rail trains.

Upon leaving St John's, the two tracks soon merge into one at Smallbrook Junction. Here on the right the line to Newport and Cowes once ran: this route closed in 1966 except for the section between Haven Street and Wooton, now operated by the Isle of Wight Steam Railway Company. It is hoped that this service will eventually run on to Smallbrook and connect into the British Rail Ryde–Shanklin line.

We now traverse the delightful Whitefield Woods where you may be lucky enough to spot a red squirrel or at dusk a friendly barn owl perched on one of the lineside fence posts. The train coasts down into the station at Brading – a village which contains much to interest the visitor and all within easy reach of the station.

The Osborne-Smith Wax Museum, set in the ancient Rectory, makes ideal entertainment whatever the weather. Alongside is the Animal World with its great colourful diaramas presenting a lifelike collection of animals, birds, and reptiles from all over the world. Near by is the Lilliput Museum of Dolls and Toys containing one of the finest and most comprehensive collections of antique dolls.

Brading also contains two famous houses: Nunwell House, where King Charles I spent his last night of freedom; and Morton Manor, an historic country house dating back to 1249 with its gardens, vineyard, and museum. Located on the Sandown side of Brading is the Roman Villa dating from the third century and once the centre of a prosperous estate. It contains restored pictorial mosaic floors with many exhibits from the original excavation. Finally, look out for the old iron ring situated in the High Street. It was traditionally used for bull-baiting and the area is still known as the 'bull-ring'.

As we leave Brading you can see from the left-hand side of the train the River Yar. We soon enter the open country of Morton Common after which the line will start its long climb that will last all the way to Shanklin.

Sandown offers many attractions to the visitor with its sandy beaches making it an ideal holiday centre. On the northern edge of town is the Isle of Wight Zoo, noted for its snake and reptile collection. Near by is a wind-surfing centre with canoes and surf-boards available for hire. At the centre of Sandown sea-front is a modern pier which includes a theatre with its star summer shows. The Sandown Bay Leisure Centre at the top of Lake Hill boasts excellent swimming facilities and squash-courts, sauna, sun-beds, and a large café all providing ideal all-weather facilities. If your flight of fancy is flying, then pleasure flights from Sandown Airport are a must.

Back at Sandown Station, you may notice a collection of wagons and perhaps a diesel locomotive. This is British Rail's Island Engineering Train, used mainly at night for track maintenance purposes. The siding that curves a short way into the distance is all that remains of the former line to Newport. Our electric train arrives, and it is time to continue our journey to Lake.

Lake Station was opened by Network South East in May 1987 with a financial contribution from the Isle of Wight County Council. It not only serves a residential area and the nearby Lake shopping centre, but is also well placed for the cliff path that runs between Sandown and Shanklin. There are marvellous views of the bay and also access via steps at various points to wonderful secluded beaches. Wight Water Adventure Sports operate from Dunroamin Beach, Lake, offering water-sport facilities for the whole family.

As we leave Lake Station, on the left we catch a glimpse of the sea as the train skirts the cliff-tops. All too soon we reach the end of our Ryde Rail journey at Shanklin. Beyond the buffer stops a new road leading to a holiday camp is built over the remains of the former railway to Ventnor, closed in 1966.

Shanklin is a famous resort and rightly so, with the railway station conveniently situated for all of its attractions. A recent innovation has been the Shanklin Pony bus service during the summer months – an open-top single-deck service operating at frequent intervals from the station yard direct to the beach, Old Village, and various hotels.

Beyond the popular shopping centre is the Old Village with its thatched cottages and its much-photographed pub, the Crab Inn. Connecting the Old Village to the beach is Shanklin Chine – a chine is a deep narrow ravine, and your walk through it will encompass a world of rare plants and dramatic waterfalls. At dusk, subtle floodlighting enhances this memorable walk still further. Shanklin Esplanade offers a sandy beach, a lift to the cliff-top but, alas, no longer a pier. This was a victim of the hurricane that struck south-eastern England in October 1987. There are, however, plans for a new pier.

If a game of cricket played in an idyllic setting takes your fancy, then the Shanklin Cricket Club ground at Westhill, a short walk from the Old Village, is a must. Games are played on a Wednesday, Saturday, and Sunday in what must surely be one of the most picturesque grounds in England.

Ryde Rail can transport you, then, to a variety of pleasures. In fact, the railway itself is a major attraction, with many motorists parking their cars at either St John's

Road, Sandown, or Shanklin in order to take their families for a trip on the Island train.

Isle of Wight Steam Railway

The year 1987 was memorable in Island railway history, for it saw the opening of two railway stations and laid the foundations for a possible third. As well as Lake, a new station was opened at Wooton by the Isle of Wight Steam Railway Company. In his opening speech on 31 May, Network South East Director Chris Green gave British Rail's support for an extension of the line to Smallbrook, where a new station would be built to allow interchange with Ryde Rail, provided that other sponsors were forthcoming.

The Haven Street–Wooton line is run entirely by volunteers. Memories are kept alive of Island steam and the relaxed air of travel in those halcyon days. The main centre at Haven Street (accessible by bus from Ryde Esplanade) includes a museum, a book and souvenir shop, and a cafeteria; not forgetting, of course, the delightful journey to Wooton, 1½ miles away, during which one can view the Island scenery at a sedate speed away from modern-day rush and tear.

The railway is always on the look-out for more members, especially if the extension to Smallbrook goes ahead. If you can help, please write to the Isle of Wight Railway Company Ltd, The Railway Station, Haven Street, Ryde, Isle of Wight PO33 4DS (telephone IOW 882204).

BROCKENHURST–LYMINGTON
by Trevor Garrod

Lymington is a pleasant town of some 35,000 people, situated at the mouth of a winding river and linked to the mainline by a 5½-mile electrified branch.

An hourly shuttle service leaves Brockenhurst Station throughout the day, with some extras at busy periods. On summer Saturdays there are some direct trains from Waterloo, and on Sundays trains run through from Eastleigh and Southampton.

The branch train, normally a four-car electric multiple unit, runs parallel to the mainline until it reaches the outskirts of Brockenhurst village, whence it heads southeastwards across open heathland. After about 1½ miles the scenery changes to woodland as the single track curves down into the river valley. To the left, down among trees, is the attractive village of Boldre. The train now crosses the main road and, at certain times, calls at Wellworthy Ampress Works Halt, which serves the adjacent factory and is not for public use.

The houses of Lymington now cover the hillside to our right; the river to our left widens into an estuary and beyond it is rising woodland. We are then soon in Lymington Town Station, a single platform with a neat brick two-storey building, refurbished in 1986 with financial help from three local authorities and two local amenity groups.

From here it is a few minutes' walk to the wide main street with its good array of shops; and the cobbled lanes that lead down to the quayside. Lymington – in the Middle Ages a port comparable to Portsmouth – is nowadays a very popular yachting centre, and as our train continues across the river we have a fine view of the boats and quay to our right. Beyond are shipyards and, at the mouth of the river, a large salt-water swimming-pool.

A large white Sealink steamer now awaits our train as we draw into Lymington Pier Station. The crossing to the Isle of Wight, whose downs loom up on the far side of the Solent, takes half an hour and operates every hour – or every half hour during the summer season. At Yarmouth, on the Island there is no longer a railway (it closed in 1952), but buses run to Freshwater and Newport (telephone Southern Vectis on IOW 522456).

CITY OF SOUTHAMPTON
by Trevor Garrod

Practically everyone has heard of Southampton as one of the major ports, not only of this country but of the world. This city of 215,000 people also boasts a university, a First Division football club, two theatres, two cinemas, three galleries, five museums, and a host of modern industries. Southampton is used to welcoming visitors – in the heyday of the ocean liner it was the gateway to England for hundreds of thousands of foreign travellers; and today it remains an ideal touring centre as well as being well worth exploring in its own right.

Southampton's historic centre was badly bombed in the Second World War, but was rebuilt soon after. As soon as you leave the station, you see on the low ridge to the east the distinctive white tower of the Civic Centre; whose style is reflected in the simple clean lines of the post-war buildings in the main north–south thoroughfare, now a shopping precinct.

Strolling up the hill from the station, and turning right into the pedestrian precinct, you can soon reach the modern and well-stocked Tourist Information Office. Your eye will also be taken by the Bargate. A few yards further down the street – called, at this point, 'Above Bargate' – is a solid medieval stone gateway that survived the bombing and contrasts sharply with the modern buildings surrounding it. Inside the Bargate is a small museum.

The main street continues – but no longer pedestrianised – as High Street, leading down to the Town Quay, past some fragments of the town wall and a ruined church. It is worth turning right, half-way down High Street, to visit the Tudor House Museum, a fine old half-timbered building in Bugle Street.

At the Town Quay is the twelfth-century God's House Tower containing a museum of archaeology; while a walk along Platform Road to the left brings you to the Eastern Docks and Ocean Village.

No visit to Southampton would be complete without a boat trip. One possibility is to take the ferry which operates at frequent intervals from the quayside across to Hythe. You should not be seasick on this fifteen-minute trip, which provides views up Southampton Water towards the Western Docks; and downstream towards the Eastern Docks and the wooded shore around Netley.

On arrival at Hythe Pier, another experience awaits you in the form of one of Hampshire's lesser-known railways. The Hythe Pier Railway is a narrow-gauge track, electrified by third rail, whose little locomotive alternately pulls or pushes three coaches along the 500-yard pier. Hythe itself is a pleasant town with waterside shops and eating-places. The bus service hence to Beaulieu and Lymington is recommended for its scenic route; as are boat trips to the Isle of Wight or the Hamble River operated by Solent Cruises (telephone 0703-843203).

For more information about the attractions of Southampton and its surroundings contact the Tourism and Conference Unit, Civic Centre, Southampton, S09 4XF.

CITY OF PORTSMOUTH
by Ken Wright

The City of Portsmouth was initially granted its charter in 1194 by Richard I, although the northern edge of the harbour was used by the Romans, since it was there that they constructed Portchester Castle. By 1185 its cathedral was founded.

In the fifteenth century the way was paved for making Portsmouth the bustling place it is today, with the construction of a dry dock, ramparts, and other defence works. From this time on it became of increasing importance to the Navy and it still remains a naval base housing all types of vessels including submarines.

Both ferry terminals at Portsmouth Harbour and Gosport are excellent vantage points for viewing the harbour and its contents and at certain times it is possible to go on a motor launch round it. On certain days of the year, particularly in August, parts of the Royal Naval Dockyard are thrown open to the public and one can see, apart from modern floating ships, both HMS *Victory* (Nelson's famous flagship at the Battle of Trafalgar in 1805) and the recently raised (1982) hull of the *Mary Rose*, a naval warship during the reign of Henry VIII. The visit is well worth while just to see these two ships alone. The *Victory* is very impressive, being kept as far as possible as it was at the time of Trafalgar, but mind your head below decks as space is confined! There is also a Royal Naval Museum in the Dockyard area.

Offshore in the Solent can clearly be seen several naval batteries and forts. These were constructed mostly between 1850 and 1860 by the then Prime Minister, Lord Palmerston, who also ordered work on fortifications on top of Portsdown Hill overlooking the city. It is somewhat ironic that this was being done to guard against a possible French invasion by Napoleon III while at the same time Britain and France were officially allied fighting the Russians in the Crimea! Because of its naval connection, Portsmouth became prime target for the Luftwaffe in the Second World War and 'Pompey' took a hammering. The area near the modern city centre in particular suffered, including the imposing Guildhall which was reconstructed out of the shell that remained after hostilities ceased.

Today the whole of Portsea Island is built up and the city of nearly 200,000 people stretches on to the 'mainland' in the north. (Tourist Information is available at Guildhall Square, telephone 0705-834092.)

Gosport (God's Port), founded by Henry de Blois in 1158, is possibly an even better place than Portsmouth to view the harbour. Near to HMS *Dolphin*, the training station for submarine crews, is an interesting museum on, appropriately enough, submarines. Exhibits include the historic *Holland I* which inadvertently sank in 1913 after being towed away for cutting.

CITY OF OXFORD
by Martin Smith

Oxford, the seat of the oldest university in Britain, is one of the major honeypots for foreign visitors on the tourist trail, and dozens of guide-books have been published describing the city in detail. It is intended here to point out some of the more curious and less-well-known features of Oxford, as well as the major university buildings.

Founded in Saxon times on an important crossing of the Thames, Oxenforde became a flourishing market town whose citizens have frequently been at loggerheads with the university which, beginning as an informal gathering of teachers and students (clerks) about 1170, became a cuckoo in the nest. There were riots between Town and Gown and an incident in 1209 known as the 'Suspendium clericorum', the 'hanging of the clerks', encouraged the university to migrate to Cambridge. The granting of a charter by the Papal Legate in 1214 enabled it to return to Oxford in safety, but some of the clerks preferred to stay in Cambridge and started a new university there.

Frequent buses run from the railway station to the city centre, but as the distance is only ½ mile, it is an easy walk with some interesting deviations. On leaving the modern station, you pass the old LN & WR station, built in 1851 from prefabricated cast-iron sections the same as the Crystal Palace. It is proposed to preserve and resurrect this structure in the redevelopment of the station site.

Take the left fork and continue along Hythe Bridge Street to the bridge crossing the Castle Mill Stream, a branch of the Thames. This was the site of the principal hythe or wharf for river traffic to Oxford in the Middle Ages. Here the Oxford Canal comes to a dead end also, since its basin was filled in. Follow the stream southwards along Upper and Lower Fisher Row, and you find yourself opposite the castle walls and the twelfth-century St George's Tower. Cross the stream into Tidmarsh Lane, turn right at the end of the lane into New Road and you come to the eleventh-century castle mound. In 1142 the Empress Matilda was besieged here by King Stephen, but this was the last occasion when the castle was subjected to military assault. By the time of the Civil War it was already ruinous and since the eighteenth century the site has been occupied by Oxford Prison, which is not open to the public.

Opposite is Nuffield College, built in 1949–60 on the site of the canal basin. Just beyond is the old canal company's offices, fronted by a Doric portico. At the top end of New Road you come to Bonn Square, a picturesque garden frequented by picturesque drunks, unfortunately. Continue through Queen Street, which is enlivened in summer by many street entertainers, and you come to the main crossroads, called Carfax (from the French *carrefour* meaning 'crossroads'). On the left stands Carfax Tower, all that remains of St Martin's Church, demolished to make way for a nineteenth-century road-widening scheme.

The High Street goes straight ahead, but turn right into St Aldate's, the departure-point for open-top bus tours of Oxford and to Blenheim. On the right is the Tourist Information Bureau (telephone 0865–726871) and on the left the florid Jacobean-style Town Hall, of which one wing houses the Museum of Oxford. This shows the history of the 'real' Oxford, from prehistory to Morris Motors. It is well worth a visit and admission is free, unlike the Oxford Museum in Broad Street, an exhibition of the history of the university, which is a commercial venture.

Farther down the hill, on the left, is Christ Church, the grandest of the Oxford colleges, founded by Cardinal Wolsey in 1525 and incorporating the twelfth-century Priory Church of St Frideswide, now the cathedral. The tower over the gateway, called Tom Tower, was added by Wren in 1681. Beyond Christ Church you come to the entrance to Christ Church Meadow, where you can enjoy a pleasant walk by the river and exit into the lower end of High Street; or leave the meadow on the north side by the exit into Merton Street and visit Oxford's oldest college, Merton, founded in 1264.

Merton Street also leads into the lower end of the High Street, where you turn right to go into Magdalen College, famous for its deer park, and the Botanic Garden which was founded in the seventeenth century as the Physick Garden, for the cultivation of medicinal plants. As you return up the High Street, the vista of its sweeping curve is dominated by the soaring spire of St Mary's Church. The ascent of the tower affords the best views of Oxford.

Here is the heart of the university and the most splendid sequence of urban architecture to be found in England. To the north of St Mary's stands the eighteenth-century domed circular library called the Radcliffe Camera. On the left is Brasenose College and on the right All Souls College with its fantastic towers designed by Hawksmoor.

Beyond the Camera is the Bodleian Library (the university library), which has had the privilege of claiming a free copy of every book published in England since 1602 and in the United Kingdom since 1814, and now has more than 5,000,000 books. Go through the Bodleian Library and you come to the Clarendon Building, built by Hawksmoor in 1711–15 to house the University Press. To the left is Wren's Sheldonian Theatre, completed in 1669, and beyond that the Old Ashmolean Museum, now the Museum of the History of Science. On the right is Hertford College with its 'Bridge of Sighs' crossing New College Lane. New College is worth a detour:

its gardens are bounded by the most complete surviving stretch of the medieval city wall, and in its fine chapel is Epstein's statue of Lazarus.

The University Museum in Parks Road houses the natural history and geological collections. Beyond its Gothic facade, with windows adorned by elaborate carving, the main exhibition room is a covered quadrangle with an iron and glass roof whose columns are decorated with exquisite wrought-iron foliage by Skidmore who later did similar work for the St Pancras Station Hotel.

Beyond the University Museum is the Pitt Rivers Museum (only open 2–4 p.m.), housing the ethnological collection, crammed with every kind of human artefact and relic from totem-poles to shrunken heads. The Ashmolean Museum (closed on Mondays) in Beaumont Street houses the university's arts and archaeological collections, and also such odd curios as Guy Fawkes's lantern and Pocahontas's cloak. The Museum of Modern Art, in a converted warehouse in Pembroke Street, plays host to travelling exhibitions of international repute.

There is much more to see, and you really need more than one day to enjoy all the riches of Oxford at leisure.

FURTHER INFORMATION

Tourist Boards
The Thames & Chilterns Tourist Board covers Berkshire, Oxfordshire, and Buckinghamshire. Its headquarters are at 8 The Market Place, Abingdon, Oxon, OX14 3UD (telephone 0235–22711). The rest of the area covered by this book is served by the Southern Tourist Board, The Old Town Hall, Leigh Road, Eastleigh, Hants, SO5 4DE (telephone 0703–616027).

Timetables and Leaflets
British Rail publish a passenger timetable for the whole country of over 1,400 pages, in May and October each year. It can be bought at staffed stations and at booksellers, and is usually available at public libraries.

Staffed stations and British Rail Travel Agents can also supply, free of charge, timetable booklets and leaflets for individual lines or groups of lines; leaflets about special offers, Railcards, taking bicycles by train, etc.

The Network Card is a Railcard for anyone over sixteen and gives one-third off leisure tickets for journeys throughout Network South East. Travel any time after 10 a.m. weekdays and when you like at week-ends. There are also discounts for children or other adults who travel with you. Ask for details at any staffed station on Network South East, which covers nearly all lines in the area of this book.

Bus Services
Deregulation of bus services was introduced under the 1986 Transport Act. As a result, information about bus services given in a guide-book of this kind may soon become out of date and we cannot accept any responsibility for changes that may have occurred since we went to press in January 1988.

However, we have given telephone numbers from which you may make enquiries in the text of various articles. You can also obtain up-to-date bus information by contacting the Transport Co-ordinating Officer of each County Council.

Canal
For further information about the Kennet & Avon Canal Trust, which has been restoring this waterway for over twenty-five years, contact them at Canal Centre, Couch Lane, Devizes, Wilts (telephone 0380–71297).

WHAT IS THE RAILWAY DEVELOPMENT SOCIETY?

It is a national, voluntary, independent body which campaigns for better rail services, for both passengers and freight, and greater use of rail transport.

It publishes books and reports, holds meetings and exhibitions, sometimes runs special trains and puts the rail-users' point of view to politicians, commerce, and industry as well as feeding users' comments and suggestions to British Rail management and unions.

There are fifteen RDS Branches, covering all of Great Britain. The Thames Valley Branch covers Berkshire, Oxfordshire, and Buckinghamshire; while the Wessex Branch covers Hampshire, the Isle of Wight, and part of Wiltshire, the rest of this county being covered by the Severnside Branch.

Membership is open to all who are in general agreement with the Society's aims and subscriptions (spring 1988) are:
Standard rate: £7.50
Pensioners, students, unemployed: £40
Families: £7.50 plus £1 for each member of household.

Write to the Membership Secretary, Mr F. J. Hastilow, 49 Irnham Road, Sutton Coldfield, West Midlands, B74 2TQ. For other information about the society and its branches, write to the General Secretary, Mr T. J. Garrod, 15 Clapham Road, Lowestoft, Suffolk, NR32 1RQ.

Local rail users' groups

There are also seventy local rail-users' groups affiliated to the RDS. Those in the region covered by this book are:

Chiltern Line Users' Association, for the two routes to Aylesbury. Secretary: Peter Clarke, 49 Risborough Road, Stoke Mandeville, Bucks.

Cotswold Line Promotion Group – formed in 1978 to publicise, safeguard, and improve rail and bus feeder services along the Oxford–Worcester line. One of the largest groups of its kind in the country, it still welcomes new members. Membership Secretary: J. E. Stanley, 4 Sandford Rise, Charlbury, Oxford, OX7 3SZ.

Marlow–Maidenhead Passengers' Association formed in 1972, soon after the closure of the Bourne End–High Wycombe section, to safeguard and promote the rest of the line. Also concerned with local bus services, and has run special trains from the branch. Contact: Mike Cooper (Publicity Officer), 67 Bradenham Road, West Wycombe, High Wycombe, Bucks, HP14 4EZ.

Oxford–Bicester Rail Users' Group formed in 1987 to promote and campaign for improvements on the newly reopened service. To join, send £1 to Membership Secretary, 25 Danes Road, Bicester, Oxon, OX6 8LL.

Newbury & District Railway Passenger Association represents the interests of rail-users along the Kennet Valley line from Theale to Pewsey. Recent achievements are the re-timing of morning trains to be more suitable for schoolchildren and saving the main morning and evening through train from Westbury. Subscription is £2, send to the Treasurer, 28 Park Lane, Thatcham, Newbury, Berks, RG13 3PJ.

ISBN 0–7117–0332–9
©1988 Railway Development Society
Published and printed in Great Britain by Jarrold and Sons Ltd, Norwich. 1/88